Brain-Sharpening
Memory Puzzles

Test Your Recall with 80 Photo Games

LUKE SHARPE

PUZZLE
WRIGHT
PRESS

New York

PUZZLE
WRIGHT
PRESS

New York

An Imprint of Sterling Publishing
1166 Avenue of the Americas
New York, NY 10036

ISBN 978-1-4549-1653-6

Distributed in Canada by Sterling Publishing
c/o Canadian Manda Group, 664 Annette Street
Toronto, Ontario, Canada M6S 2C8
Distributed in the United Kingdom by GMC Distribution Services
Castle Place, 166 High Street, Lewes, East Sussex, England BN7 1XU
Distributed in Australia by Capricorn Link (Australia) Pty. Ltd.
P.O. Box 704, Windsor, NSW 2756, Australia

For information about custom editions, special sales, and premium and
corporate purchases, please contact Sterling Special Sales at 800-805-5489 or
specialsales@sterlingpublishing.com.

Manufactured in China

4 6 8 10 9 7 5

www.puzzlewright.com

Contents

Introduction

How much do we really remember of what we see? The human brain is an amazing thing, but its memory may be less reliable than we think. Many overturned criminal convictions were originally based on the testimony of eyewitnesses who were confident that they remembered things a certain way, but were later proven wrong.

In this book, you'll get to find out just how well your memory works (and how much it improves by the end). On each right-hand page, there is a picture to study and an icon indicating the time limit, from three to six minutes. Photos that are oriented vertically and photos oriented horizontally are separated into their own sections, so you don't have to keep rotating the book as you go through it; within each section, the difficulty increases as you continue, as does the time limit. After examining the picture for the full amount of time, turn the page over; on the opposite side is a set of questions about the picture, ranging from easy to difficult. Some of the questions will ask about obvious features of the picture, and some will ask about small details.

For example, take a look at the picture below. This photo is less detailed than the real puzzles, so don't take more than a minute to study it, if you'd like to try answering the sample questions on the next page.

An easy question I might ask about that picture is "True or false: Both people in the picture are wearing hats." Medium-difficulty questions might be "What is the name of the memory course?" and "On which finger of which hand has the man tied a string?" Finally, a hard question might be "How many buttons of the man's vest are unbuttoned?" Easy questions are worth 1 point, medium questions are worth 3 points, and hard questions are worth 5 points. Some questions have bonus points available; for instance, the third question above might have asked, "On which finger of which hand has the man tied a string (and, for a bonus point, is it the same finger as the one shown on the sign)?" Even if you don't answer the main question correctly, you can still earn the bonus points, unless otherwise specified in the question.

You can always check your answers by going back to look at the picture again, but you may find it easier to simply consult the back of the book. (The correct answers to the above questions are, respectively: true; the Nu-System Memory Course; the right thumb, which is the same finger as shown on the sign; and one button.)

If you would like an extra challenge, you can increase the difficulty in one of two ways (earning extra points accordingly). You may reduce the time you study the picture; for each minute by which you reduce the time limit, you earn an extra 3 points, but to collect each minute's points you must answer at least one question correctly. So, for instance, if you study a picture with a 6-minute time limit for 3 minutes, but then answer only two questions correctly, you only earn 6 bonus points, not 9. Alternately, you may study the picture for the full amount of time ... and then step away from the book for a while before answering the questions. For each minute you wait between studying the photo and answering the questions, you earn 3 bonus points (but, as before, must answer at least one correct answer per minute to collect the extra points).

For *less* of a challenge, you may increase the time limit, subtracting 3 points from your overall score for each minute you add.

That's about all you need to know. Don't forget to enjoy yourself!

—Luke Sharpe

3 min.

WE BUY AT
WE SELL AT
AUSTRALIA AUD
BRAZIL BRL
CANADA CAD
CHINA CNY
EUROPEAN UNION EUR
JAPAN JPY
MEXICO MXP
NORWAY NOK
RUSSIA RR
SWEDEN SEK
SWITZERLAND CHF
UNITED KINGDOM GBP

For convenience, all entities that appear on the board in the preceding image will be referred to below as "countries."

Easy questions (1 point):

1) True or false: Japan's unit of currency has the lowest value.

2) True or false: The date display in the upper left reads "04-08"

Medium questions (3 points):

3) What time is it?

4) Which country's readout is not lit?

5) What country's currency abbreviation is only two letters long?

6) How many countries' "We buy at" amounts are greater than $1.00?

7) How many countries on the board have flags colored red and white (and no other color)? For 3 bonus points, name them all. (If you can only name some of them, subtract 1 bonus point for each one you leave out.)

Hard questions (5 points):

8) For 5 points each, name the three-letter currency abbreviation that precedes each of the following on the board:
   a) EUR
   b) BRL
   c) NOK
   d) JPY

9) Which two countries' currency abbreviations do not start with the same letter as their names?

10) Two adjacent countries on the board have red, white, and blue flags. Name them.

Your score: _____
Maximum base score: 50
Answers, page 167

Easy questions (1 point):

1) True or false: The clown's right foot (on your left) is tilted up.

2) True or false: The billboard in the lower right is surrounded with lights.

Medium questions (3 points):

3) What is the name of the theme park? (And for a bonus point, how many "family fun attractions" does it feature?)

4) Which letter at the top of the sign does not have a lit-up border, and what word is it part of?

5) How many photographs of theme park rides are there?

6) What are the main colors of the background and banner in the theme park ad?

7) For 3 points each, fill in the missing words below:
   a) Vince Neil's _____
   b) Free _____ circus acts daily

8) Which of the following best describes the shape of the clown's pupils?
   a) circle
   b) heart
   c) square
   d) triangle

Hard questions (5 points):

9) Which of the following correctly describes Vince Neil (pictured in the advertisement for his restaurant)?
   a) wearing sunglasses, holding a drink in his right hand
   b) wearing sunglasses, holding a drink in his left hand
   c) not wearing sunglasses, holding a drink in his right hand
   d) not wearing sunglasses, holding a drink in his left hand

10) How many red semicircular sections are there in the lollipop that the clown is holding?

11) In the slogan "Eat, Drink, Party," what are the widest letters in each of the three words?

12) What is the name of the restaurant advertised on the billboard in the lower right?

Your score: _____
Maximum base score: 44
Answers, page 167

Easy questions (1 point):

1) True or false: Of the people depicted on the stamps, all have been president of the United States.

2) Which of the following is the first name of at least one person depicted on the stamps?
   a) Theodore
   b) James
   c) Andrew
   d) John

Medium questions (3 points):

3) What is depicted on the stamp in the upper left? (And for an extra point, what is its value?)

4) Whose image appears on the most stamps? (And for 3 extra points, what is the total value of the stamps on which he appears?)

5) Where is the green stamp?

6) Who is the only person depicted wearing glasses?

7) Whose image appears on the stamp with the lowest value?

8) What state abbreviation appears on the stamp in the upper right?

Hard questions (5 points):

9) One stamp features two presidents' names; name them both.

10) Two stamps have the same value; whose images appear on those stamps?

11) If the stamps were a tic-tac-toe board, which three in a line would have the lowest value, and what is that value?

12) All the stamps but one include the words "United States Postage." What appears on the remaining stamp in place of that phrase, and what is that stamp's location?

13) Two stamps' values are two-digit numbers. What is the total value of those two stamps?

Your score: _____
Maximum base score: 49
Answers, page 167

Easy questions (1 point):

1) True or false: There are three carrots pictured.

2) True or false: The bread is resting on a plate.

3) What is the four-word phrase at the top of the poster?

Medium questions (3 points):

4) In the carton of eggs, three eggs are partly colored orange. How are they arranged?
   a) in an orthogonal line
   b) in a diagonal line
   c) not in a line

5) How many words in the paragraph below the illustration are in all caps? Also, two pairs of the words begin with the same letter; give yourself a bonus point for each pair you can name.

6) How many radishes are pictured?

7) What two items extend past the top of the blue oval?

8) What vegetable is on the plate with the steak and french fries?

Hard questions (5 points):

9) One word in the paragraph below the illustration is broken up across two lines with a hyphen. What word?

10) How many eggs are recommended to be eaten in a week?

11) How many yellow lines are visible on the front of the cereal box?

12) Place the following items in the order in which they appear in the paragraph below the illustration:
    a) white flour
    b) grapefruit
    c) nuts
    d) tomatoes

Your score: _____
Maximum base score: 40
Answers, page 167

Easy questions (1 point):

1) True or false: It costs 10 baht to use a locker.

2) Which locker is the only one without a key?

Medium questions (3 points):

3) What are the numbers of the two lockers whose handles do not have "Pull" stickers on them?

4) What are the two English words at the top of the sticker on the upper right locker? (And for a bonus point, what is that locker's number?)

5) How many locker numbers are divisible by three?

6) For 3 points each, fill in the missing words below:
   a) _____ key-attached locker (two words)
   b) Turn the key _____ & pull out the key
   c) Key lost, contact _____ at once

7) What is the difference between the first two locker numbers in the top row?

Hard questions (5 points):

8) Which three lockers' numbers are visible on the yellow circles attached to their keys?

9) How many Thai characters appear on the same line as the phrase "How to lock"?

10) Which numbered sticker's upper right corner is peeling off?

Your score: _____
Maximum base score: 39
Answers, page 167

Easy questions (1 point):

1) True or false: The M&M's on the shelf above the magazines are plain.

2) Over how many cartoons are in the magazine to the right of Vogue?

Medium questions (3 points):

3) What word is at the top of the sign with the price $2.59?

4) What celebrity is mentioned on the cover of Vogue below the Lena Dunham headline?

5) What is the price of gum?

6) What brand of gum is oriented differently than the other brands?

7) What month's issue is the Vogue magazine?

8) What candy is to the right of the 100 Grand bars?

9) How many different brands of candy bar have the phrase "2 to Go" printed on their labels?

Hard questions (5 points):

10) How many sticks of gum are in a pack?

11) What is the weight of the Snickers bar (in ounces or grams)?

Your score: _____
Maximum base score: 33
Answers, page 167

Easy questions (1 point):

1) True or false: Every postcard with oranges also depicts orange blossoms.

2) True or false: The Mexican border can be seen on the map.

3) Which of the following cities' names is not fully visible on the map?
   a) Los Angeles
   b) Fresno
   c) Long Beach
   d) San Diego

Medium questions (3 points):

4) How many postcards can be seen in the photo?

5) According to its postcard, what is the nickname of Santa Catalina Island?

6) Which postcard has no other postcards on top of it?

7) On the Yosemite National Park postcard, which of the letters in "Yosemite" is the tallest?

8) Which postcard includes the phrase "and Vicinity"?

9) How many flowers are visible on the "Sunny Southern California" postcard?

Hard questions (5 points):

10) How many islands are fully visible on the map?

11) One postcard includes the word "Redwood" twice. What two words immediately follow it?

12) What two locations' postcards include the word "scenic"?

Your score: _____
Maximum base score: 36
Answers, page 167

Easy questions (1 point):

1) True or false: The jackpot is between $943,000 and $944,000.

2) What color are the numbers of the 1000 value on the wheel?

Medium questions (3 points):

3) What word is seen on the center of the large wheel?

4) Which of the following values is not seen among the "1st Credit Winners" and "2nd Credit Winners"?
   a) 200
   b) 400
   c) 2000
   d) 4000

5) What is the second-largest value on the wheel? (And for 2 bonus points, what color is it?)

6) What is the lowest value on the wheel? (And for 2 bonus points, what color is it?)

7) In the jackpot, what is the rightmost digit that is not changing?

Hard questions (5 points):

8) What is the "1st Credit" prize for spinning three 7's?

9) How many sections are there on the large wheel?

10) Place the colors associated on the payout tables with triple bars, double bars, single bar, and "any bar" in order by their positions on the display, from top to bottom:
   a) blue
   b) purple
   c) white
   d) yellow

Your score: _____
Maximum base score: 36
Answers, page 167

Easy questions (1 point):

1) True or false: The speed limit is 25.

2) True or false: The figures on the "Caution" sign are all holding hands.

3) What color is the traffic light in the foreground?

4) What is the full name of the street whose sign is visible?

Medium questions (3 points):

5) How many signs feature a "no" symbol (a red circle with a line through it)?

6) During what hours is there no turn on red?

7) What two things are prohibited by the sign below the one reading "Speed checked by radar"?

8) On what day of the month does street sweeping take place?

9) For 3 points each, indicate whether the following descriptions apply to the left-hand pole, the center pole, or the right-hand pole:
   a) the pole with the most signs
   b) the pole with the most red on its signs
   c) the pole with the highest sign

Hard questions (5 points):

10) What is the number of the highway on the sign that can be seen behind the fence?

11) In the foreground of the photo, there are four signs with colored backgrounds— that is, a color besides black or white. List the four colors in order from top to bottom.

12) What is the address number on the street sign?

13) What two words follow this text from the blue sign: "Unauthorized vehicles not displaying ..."?

14) How many arrows are visible on the signs in the foreground?

15) Of those arrows, some are pointing in the same direction. How many, and which direction?

Your score: _____
Maximum base score: 55
Answers, page 167

Easy questions (1 point):

1) True or false: The bow that Minnie Mouse is wearing on the upper candy tin is identical to the one she is wearing on the lower tin.

2) On which tin is a character wearing glasses?

Medium questions (3 points):

3) What two colors are the stars on Donald Duck's candy tins?

4) What word is in the speech balloon in the upper left candy tin? (Spelling counts!)

5) On the lower set of candy tins, which two signatures are in cursive? (And for an extra point, which signature is not written in black or white?)

6) On which of the eight candy tins are no punctuation marks visible?

7) On how many tins is the depicted character's left hand not even partially visible?

Hard questions (5 points):

8) Which two of the tins have question marks printed on them?

9) The four lower "Oh sweet" balloons are each shaped either like a starburst or a cloud. Correctly identify all four, from left to right.

10) On which of the eight candy tins is a character holding his or her hands together?

11) Which two tins depict a character holding a hand to his or her mouth?

12) How many exclamation points in total appear on all eight tins?

Your score: _____
Maximum base score: 43
Answers, page 168

Easy questions (1 point):

1) True or false: There are 20 visible sets of items available in the vending machine.

2) Which of the following items is not available for purchase?
   a) Planters Peanuts
   b) Clif Bar
   c) Twix
   d) Slim Jim

Medium questions (3 points):

3) How much would it cost to buy one item from each of the top three rows?

4) How many even-numbered items are visible?

5) Name either of the two items that are directly below the package of BelVita. (For 2 bonus points, name both.)

6) What is the name of the mouse on the packaging for Herr's Baked Cheese Curls?

Hard questions (5 points):

7) What are the three Nabisco products?

8) What number item is a pack of Snyder's Mini Pretzels?

9) What are the two flavors of Kar's snack mix that are available?

10) What is the brand of the item that says it contains "No Trans Fats"?

Your score: _____
Maximum base score: 36
Answers, page 168

Easy questions (1 point):

1) True or false: The top left drawer is labeled "Astronomy – Botany."

2) Which language appears on one of the labels?
   a) Danish
   b) Dutch
   c) Finnish
   d) French

Medium questions (3 points):

3) What drawer number has a crooked label?

4) What is on the label on the drawer two to the left of "Geology – History"?

5) How many visible screws hold in place each drawer's handle?

6) What misspelled word completes the label "English – _____"?

7) What is the sum of the drawer numbers in the third row?

8) How many labels span more than one letter of the alphabet?

Hard questions (5 points):

9) How many times does the word "Engineering" appear in the image?

10) Three drawers have just one word on their labels. Name them.

11) What is the label on drawer #14?

Your score: _____
Maximum base score: 35
Answers, page 168

HOW TO DIE BEFORE YOUR TIME *or* THIS IS THE WAY TO CATCH

The "Flu"

4 min.

Wear slacks all summer but come winter, take them off.

Be sure to make a pig of yourself. Eat starches. Fruit juices give you too many vitamins.

Make plenty of whoopee. It builds up business for the undertaker.

Sneeze in the other guy's face. He'll get sick, too.

Sleep open in the open. It's sure to kill you sooner.

Last of all, doctor yourself. MD's are dumb birds.

9 Rules for Fight on Flu and Colds

Remember these nine rules laid down by the epidemics committee of the Academy of Medicine of Cleveland for combating colds and influenza.

AVOID crowds.

CANCEL all unnecessary meetings.

SLEEP sufficiently.

AVOID overwork.

MAINTAIN a well-balanced diet.

TREAT every apparent cold or fever as if it were influenza.

GO TO BED at first sign of a cold or fever.

ISOLATE any patient and keep and wash his dishes separately.

DON'T RETURN to work too soon.

WPB LABOR-MANAGEMENT SAFETY-HEALTH COMMITTEE.

Addressograph-Multigraph Corp.
CLEVELAND 17, OHIO.

31

Easy questions (1 point):

1) True or false: The woman in the skirt in the top drawing on the left has a kerchief with hearts on it.

2) How many "Rules for Fight on Flu and Colds" are listed?

Medium questions (3 points):

3) What six words come before "or" in the headline at the top?

4) What word is connected by a hyphen to "Multigraph" in the name of the corporation that made this poster?

5) What two-word sentence appears between the sentences "Be sure to make a pig of yourself" and "Fruit juices give you too many vitamins"?

6) What is the word used to indicate a sneezing sound? (Spelling counts!)

7) What is the letter in a circle on the bed of the sleeping man?

8) For 3 points each, complete these ways to catch the flu:
   a) "Make plenty of whoopee. It builds up business for the _____."
   b) "Last of all, doctor yourself. MD's are _____." (two words)

Hard questions (5 points):

9) Which of these is the correct description of the drawing of the man eating?
   a) The waiter is holding a plate in his left hand and the man is holding a fork in his left hand
   b) The waiter is holding a plate in his left hand and the man is holding a fork in his right hand
   c) The waiter is holding a plate in his right hand and the man is holding a fork in his left hand
   d) The waiter is holding a plate in his right hand and the man is holding a fork in his right hand

10) In the rules in the lower right, one word is in all capital letters twice. What word is that?

11) What number appears between Cleveland and Ohio at the bottom of the poster?

12) How many shoes (including boots) can be seen on the poster?

Your score: _____
Maximum base score: 43
Answers, page 168

32

Easy questions (1 point):

1) True or false: The roulette wheel pocket #5 (as well as the "5" on the felt) is red.

2) In what numbered pocket on the roulette wheel is the white ball?

Medium questions (3 points):

3) The box labeled "1st 12" separates what two betting boxes from the numbered grid?

4) Only one bet on the board is a single chip. What color is it?

5) A stack of black chips and a stack of pink chips are each placed on intersections of four numbers. What two numbers do they have in common?

6) Green has bets in two places, one of which is on an individual number. What number?

7) Orange has a bet on the intersection of four numbers. Just one of those numbers is red. What is that red number?

8) By the roulette wheel are stacks of chips for paying out winners. What color are the stacks of chips on the left?

9) What word precedes "0/2/3" in the smaller grid?

10) What number (between 3 and 0) is on the tip of the curve of that smaller grid?

Hard questions (5 points):

11) Pink has bets in three places: an intersection of four numbers and what two individual numbers? (Give yourself 3 points if you remember only one of them.)

12) Purple has bets in two places: one on the side of the intersection of 4 and 7 (indicating a bet on 4/5/6/7/8/9) and one on what four-number intersection?

13) What number did white bet on in two separate bets?

14) Just one number in the second 12 (13 to 24) has no bet on it. That is, no chip is placed anywhere in the box or on its border. What number is it?

15) Name either number next to the 1 on the roulette wheel. (For a bonus point, name both.)

Your score: _____
Maximum base score: 52
Answers, page 168

Easy questions (1 point):

1) True or false: The Apple logo on the cover of Mac Life magazine is colored green.

2) What celebrity's nickname appears in the upper left corner of the photo?
   a) Jennifer Lopez
   b) Christina Aguilera
   c) Kanye West
   d) Rihanna

Medium questions (3 points):

3) What magazine is upside down in the rack?

4) Which of the following cover lines does not appear somewhere in the photo?
   a) Beautiful Cars
   b) Eat to Win
   c) Miley's Boy Toy
   d) Paint Prep

5) What word is prominently featured in a yellow banner on MMA magazine?

6) For 3 points each:
   a) What magazine is directly above Cycle World?
   b) What magazine is directly to the right of Cycle World?
   c) What magazine is directly to the left of Consumer Reports?
   d) What magazine is directly below MMA magazine?

7) How many faces can be seen on the cover of OK! magazine?

Hard questions (5 points):

8) How many copies of the cooking magazine at the top of the spinning rack are visible?

9) For 5 points each, what numbers are missing from the following cover lines?
   a) _____ Awesome Things Your Mac Can Do
   b) Best of the Year: _____+ Great Choices
   c) _____ Easy Summer Recipes
   d) How I Lost _____ Lbs.

Your score: _____
Maximum base score: 51
Answers, page 168

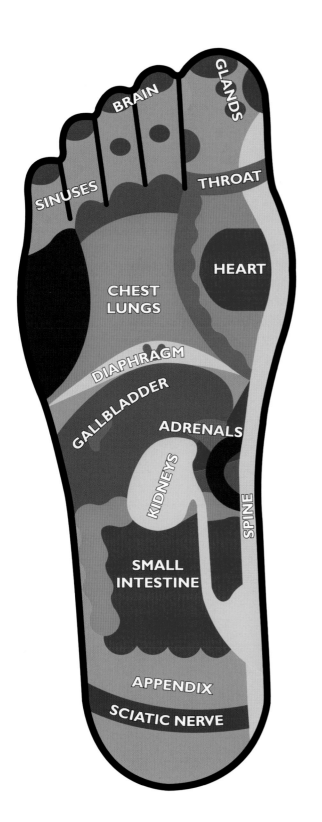
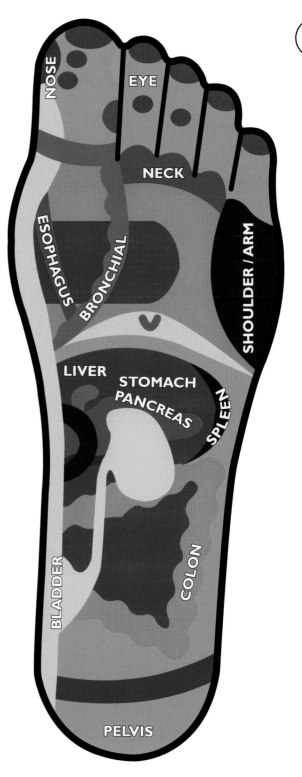

Easy questions (1 point):

1) True or false: The big toes are labeled "glands" and "eye."

2) What color is the background for "kidneys"?

Medium questions (3 points):

3) What is located below the area marked "appendix"?

4) What word appears in an orange area in the foot illustration on the right?

5) What two words are separated by a slash?

6) For 3 points each, are the following words in the foot illustration on the left or the one on the right?
a) brain
b) diaphragm
c) liver
d) neck
e) pancreas

7) What are the two smallest toes of the foot illustration on the left labeled with?

8) What is the bottom area of the foot illustration on the right labeled with?

Hard questions (5 points):

9) On the foot illustration on the right, to the right of "stomach" is a crescent-shaped area. What is it labeled?

10) What is the only four-syllable word on the foot illustration on the right?

11) Three words on the foot illustration on the left become new words when their first letters are moved to the end. One of them is "small" (from "small intestine"), which becomes "malls." What are the other two words?

Your score: _____
Maximum base score: 47
Answers, page 168

IF YOU GO INTO THE FOREST YOU MUST BE ACCOMPANIED BY AN ASSISTANT OR A GUIDE.
JIKA PERGI KE HUTAN HARUS BERSAMA DENGAN KARYAWAN ATAU GUIDE.

FOR YOUR SAFETY AND THE SAFETY OF OTHERS, PLEASE KEEP A SAFE DISTANCE FROM THE ORANGUTANS (APPROXIMATELY 5 METERS)
UNTUK KESELAMATAN DIRI SINDIRI DAN ORANG LAIN MOHON INGAT JARAK AMAN ANDA DARI ORANGUTAN (KIRA-KIRA 5 METER)

PLEASE DO NOT EAT OR DRINK IN FRONT OF THE ORANGUTANS. KEEP FOOD AND DRINKS IN YOUR BAGS.
MOHON JANGAN MAKAN ATAU MINUM DI DEPAN ORANGUTAN SIMPANLAH MINUMAN DAN MAKANAN DI DALAM TAS ANDA.

PLEASE DO NOT TOUCH OR DISTURB THE ORANGUTANS.
JANGAN MENYENTUH DAN MENGGANGU ORANGUTAN.

NEVER STAND BETWEEN A MALE AND A FEMALE ORANGUTAN
JANGAN BERADA DI ANTARA ORANGUTAN JANTAN DAN BETINA

DO NOT APPROACH OR CLIMB ON THE FEEDING PLATFORM
JANGAN MENDEKATI ATAU NAIK KE PANGGUNG

PLEASE TAKE YOUR RUBBISH (INCLUDING CIGARETTE BUTTS) WITH YOU.
BAWALAH SAMPAH (TERMASUK PUNTUNG ROKOK) BERSAMA ANDA.

Easy questions (1 point):

1) True or false: There are seven warning signs.

2) What is the predominant color of the background?

Medium questions (3 points):

3) What should you never stand between?

4) Complete the rule: "Do not approach or climb on the _____."

5) How many sets of parentheses are there on all the signs (including both the English and Indonesian warnings)?

6) How do you say "approximately" in Indonesian?

7) Three of the English warnings begin with the same word. What is that word?

Hard questions (5 points):

8) Three of the Indonesian warnings begin with the same word. What is that word?

9) On all the signs, how many instances of the word "orangutan" or "orangutans" are there?

10) What Indonesian word is partially obscured by a post?

11) What two English words besides "orangutan" appear in the Indonesian warnings?

Your score: _____
Maximum base score: 37
Answers, page 168

Easy questions (1 point):

1) True or false: The clock's minute hand is pointing to the 10.

2) Which of these cities is not listed?
   a) Athens
   b) Baghdad
   c) Cairo
   d) Denver

Medium questions (3 points):

3) What does it say above the dashed line?

4) What two-digit number is made up of a light digit and a dark digit?

5) What city shares a line with Santiago?

6) Kabul's line is pointing to what number?

7) What continent is the plane over?

Hard questions (5 points):

8) Two lines have three cities on them. Name either set. (For 5 bonus points, name both sets.)

9) What city appears between Suva/Auckland and Agana/Sydney?

10) What city is directly opposite the line with Rio de Janeiro and Buenos Aires?

11) The southern tip of South America is closest to what number?

Your score: _____
Maximum base score: 42
Answers, page 168

Easy questions (1 point):

1) True or false: The order of chicken tenders shown on the right contains 20 pieces.

2) What does it say on the sign beneath the menu on the red beam?

Medium questions (3 points):

3) What three ingredients are listed for the California Whopper?

4) How many pieces come in the BK Chicken Fries meal?

5) What is the new product that can be ordered with "burger or chicken"?

6) Which sandwich is shown with a Diet Coke?

7) What does it cost to "Go large"?

8) What are the names of the $2 and $3 sandwiches on the right side of the menu?

Hard questions (5 points):

9) What is meal #10?

10) What is the highest price shown on the menu?

11) How many of the value meals (the 12 numbered photos on the left) show Sprite as the drink?

12) What is the name of the sandwich in the lowest-numbered value meal that doesn't include the word "Whopper"?

Your score: _____
Maximum base score: 40
Answers, page 169

Easy questions (1 point):

1) True or false: The two red sections of sidewalk are touching each other.

2) True or false: The imprint of George Burns's cigar is between his handprints.

Medium questions (3 points):

3) What celebrity's name contains an "i" dotted with a star?

4) Who is the mayor whose name is seen in the upper left?

5) In the area with three adjacent black sidewalk sections, which of the four prints in the center section (initialed B.P. for Brad Pitt) is highest?
   a) left hand
   b) right hand
   c) left foot
   d) right foot

6) For 3 points each, name the year in which the following celebrities signed their names. (For 2 bonus points each, give the full date.)
   a) Burt Reynolds
   b) Peter O'Toole
   c) Cecil B. deMille

7) For 3 points each, fill in the missing words in the inscriptions below:
   a) Sid dear—My wish is for _____
      (two words)
   b) _____—I'm "Going in Style"
   c) To the public who _____
      (four words)
   d) For _____ years (two words)

Hard questions (5 points):

8) Whose footprints appear entirely to the left of that person's handprints?

9) Which two celebrities' names are written between their handprints and footprints?

10) What two celebrities share the same sidewalk section?

Your score: _____
Maximum base score: 53
Answers, page 169

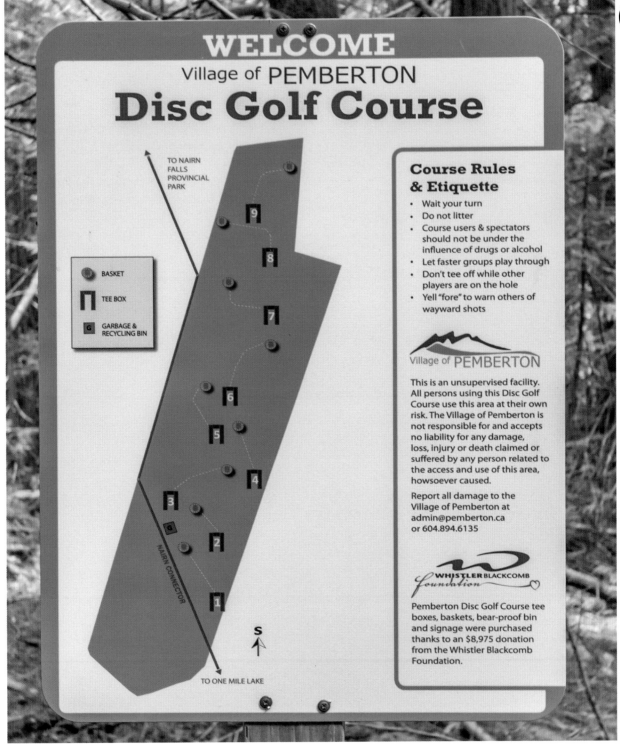

WELCOME

Village of PEMBERTON

Disc Golf Course

TO NAIRN
FALLS
PROVINCIAL
PARK

BASKET

TEE BOX

G GARBAGE &
RECYCLING BIN

9

8

7

6

5

4

3

G

2

1

S

NAIRN CONNECTOR

TO ONE MILE LAKE

Course Rules & Etiquette

- Wait your turn
- Do not litter
- Course users & spectators should not be under the influence of drugs or alcohol
- Let faster groups play through
- Don't tee off while other players are on the hole
- Yell "fore" to warn others of wayward shots

Village of PEMBERTON

This is an unsupervised facility. All persons using this Disc Golf Course use this area at their own risk. The Village of Pemberton is not responsible for and accepts no liability for any damage, loss, injury or death claimed or suffered by any person related to the access and use of this area, howsoever caused.

Report all damage to the Village of Pemberton at admin@pemberton.ca or 604.894.6135

WHISTLER BLACKCOMB
foundation

Pemberton Disc Golf Course tee boxes, baskets, bear-proof bin and signage were purchased thanks to an $8,975 donation from the Whistler Blackcomb Foundation.

Easy questions (1 point):

1) True or false: The distance from tee box 5 to tee box 6 is less than the distance from tee box 6 to tee box 7.

2) How many holes are on the disc golf course?

Medium questions (3 points):

3) What is the name of the village where the course is set?

4) What tee box is closest to the garbage & recycling bin?

5) What is the top item in the map's key?

6) What is the name of the nearby lake?

7) How many bullet points are there under the "Course Rules & Etiquette"?

8) What hyphenated adjective describes the bin?

9) What shape is connected to the "n" of "Foundation" in the Whistler Blackcomb Foundation logo?

Hard questions (5 points):

10) What two rules are three words?

11) What is the direction from tee box 7 to tee box 8?

12) What is the email address or the phone number to report damage?

13) What was the dollar amount of the donation from Whistler Blackcomb Foundation?

Your score: _____
Maximum base score: 43
Answers, page 169

5 min.

Easy questions (1 point):

1) True or false: Kate's garment in the Daily Mail photograph is purple.

2) What is the name of the bottom newspaper?

Medium questions (3 points):

3) What day of the week was the Daily Mail printed?

4) In what country were both The Sun and the Daily Express printed?

5) How much does the Daily Mail cost?

6) What is the figure in the Daily Express logo holding in front of his body?

7) How much money can you save at Smyths if you buy The Sun?

8) For 3 points each, complete these headlines:
   a) Daily Mail: "Anxious William at pregnant Kate's bedside after dramatic _____" (two words)
   b) Daily Express: "_____ for Kate & Wills" (two words)
   c) Bottom newspaper: "Mongolia gets first _____" (two words)

9) What color is the background of the Daily Express's main headline (the one that ends "for Kate & Wills")?

Hard questions (5 points):

10) What artist has a show going to Italy, according to the bottom newspaper?

11) What three words appear on a red background on the Daily Express?

12) Complete this analogy, which was created from Sun headlines: Wills : Dad :: Child : _____

Your score: _____
Maximum base score: 44
Answers, page 169

5 min.

AUTOSLOT

13:03

£0.00

PLEASE NOTE
NEW CHARGES

5p 10p 20p 50p £1

NO CHANGE GIVEN   COINS ACCEPTED

1. INSERT COINS
2. PRESS FOR TICKET

£1 FOR EACH 30 MINS

4 Hours Max

Hours of Operation
Monday – Saturday 8·30 am – 6·30 pm
Other hours Sunday & Public Holidays
no charges, no maximum stay period.

PAY AND DISPLAY PARKING

INSTRUCTIONS

1. INSERT COIN(S) TO VALUE REQUIRED.
2. ALLOW COIN(S) TO REGISTER
3. PRESS TICKET ISSUE BUTTON.
4. ATTACH TICKET TO INSIDE OF WINDSCREEN

NO CHANGE GIVEN

If this machine is out of order please purchase
a ticket from another machine if available

CONDITIONS OF USE

✳ A CONTRAVENTION occurs if during the controlled hrs
● a vehicle is parked without payment and display of a
valid ticket or overstays the expiry time shown on
a ticket.
● a ticket is not purchased at the time of parking.
● a subsequent ticket is purchased.
● a ticket is transferred to/from another vehicle.
● a vehicle returns to this parking place within one
hour of leaving.
● a vehicle parks whilst a parking bay is suspended.
● a vehicle is not parked fully in a marked bay.

✳ A PENALTY CHARGE may be incurred if a CONTRAVENTION
occurs
✳ Vehicles in CONTRAVENTION may be towed away or
wheelclamped.
✳ It is a CRIMINAL OFFENCE to insert any object other
than the specified coins.
✳ During the controlled hours vehicles displaying a valid
residents permit for Zone A2 may park free of
charge

REJECTED COINS

Easy questions (1 point):

1) True or false: Change is given.

2) Is the coin slot horizontal or vertical?

3) Are the hinges on the left or the right?

Medium questions (3 points):

4) What time is displayed?

5) What color is the background of the message "Please note new charges"?

6) What five coins are accepted?

7) What two words are at the bottom?

8) What three words are next to the "2." above the green button?

9) What are the hours of operation from Monday to Saturday?

10) Which of these contraventions is listed last on the left side of the conditions of use?
   a) a subsequent ticket is purchased
   b) a ticket is transferred to/from another vehicle
   c) a vehicle is not parked fully in a marked bay
   d) a vehicle returns to this parking place within one hour of leaving

Hard questions (5 points):

11) How much would it cost to park for the maximum allowable time during the hours of operation?

12) How many asterisks are there? And for an additional 5 points, how many bullets are there?

13) Vehicles in contravention may be towed away or what?

14) Vehicles displaying a valid residents permit for what may park free of charge?

15) What eight-letter word is at the top?

16) Complete instruction #4: "Attach ticket to _____" (three words)

Your score: _____
Maximum base score: 59
Answers, page 169

Easy questions (1 point):

1) True or false: On the card on which a word is written on a blackboard, the word is "Congratulations!"

2) Which of the following cartoon characters does not appear on at least one of the cards?
   a) Schroeder
   b) Snoopy
   c) Mickey Mouse
   d) Goofy

Medium questions (3 points):

3) One card is an audio card. Name its category.

4) Two cards indicate how much they cost. What are their prices? (And for 3 bonus points each, what are their categories?)

5) What animal is painting the graffiti "You suc..." on a wall on one card?

6) For 3 points each, complete the text of the following cards:
   a) "So long. I wish you luck. I wish you _____."
   b) "Thanks! What you did _____ ..." (four words)
   c) "A wish for you _____" (four words)

7) What two words can complete the category "Good-Bye — _____"?

8) What two categories of cards have a "Peer" subcategory?

Hard questions (5 points):

9) For 5 points each, name the category of the following cards based on a description of elements that appear on them:
   a) a butterfly
   b) a single shooting star
   c) two sunflowers whose petals form the top border of the card
   d) Winnie-the-Pooh climbing a tree

10) What is the text on the card immediately to the right of the card featuring a four-leaf clover?

Your score: _____
Maximum base score: 57
Answers, page 169

Easy questions (1 point):

1) True or false: The only license plate from a Canadian province is from British Columbia.

2) What make of motorcycle appears on the gas pump?

Medium questions (3 points):

3) One license plate is a Centennial plate with a "76" logo on it. What state is that plate from?

4) What is the price of gas per gallon, according to the pump? (Round down to the nearest whole number.)

5) A license plate from what state is directly above the circular top of the gas pump?

6) What color sticker appears on Puerto Rico's license plate (and for a bonus point, in which corner)?

7) What is the license plate number of the plate that has boats in the background?

8) Complete this sentence from the gas pump: "Glass must be _____" (five words).

Hard questions (5 points):

9) Three horizontally adjacent license plates indicate that they are truck plates. What states are those plates from? (For 2 bonus points, name the state of the one other truck plate pictured.)

10) Outlines of what three states, territories, or provinces can be seen on three license plates? (Give yourself 3 points if you can name two of the three.)

11) All of the following license plate numbers appear somewhere in the photo except one. Which is the odd one out?
a) 4PQL179
b) 97375 P
c) BF 8450
d) KDK 437

12) Place the following license plates in order from top to bottom:
a) Utah (blue plate)
b) Utah (white plate)
c) Wyoming (black plate)
d) Wyoming (yellow plate)

Your score: _____
Maximum base score: 43
Answers, page 169

Easy questions (1 point):

1) True or false: One button depicts Ronald Reagan behind a red "No" symbol.

2) One slogan (on several buttons) is written on a picture of a hat. What is the slogan?

Medium questions (3 points):

3) Three of the four people below are depicted on a button together. Which is the odd one out?
   a) Walter Mondale
   b) Geraldine Ferraro
   c) Gary Hart
   d) Jesse Jackson

4) What two candidates are depicted on the heart-shaped campaign button?

5) What toy is depicted on one of the buttons?

6) Some buttons depict people or groups of people who were not presidential candidates. For 3 points each, identify the following:
   a) a popular singer
   b) a sports team
   c) a group of three men (name their occupation)
   d) a fictional character

7) For 3 points each, complete the following buttons' slogans:
   a) _____ is worth the risk: Clinton '96
   b) Carter's Little _____ (two words)
   c) Nixon is a good _____
   d) The man for the _____

Hard questions (5 points):

8) Two candidates' buttons have slogans that begin "If I were 21, I'd vote for …"; which two? (Give yourself 2 points if you can name one of them.)

9) Which two of the following four buttons include an image of an American flag?
   a) Anderson for President
   b) Win With Johnson
   c) Wallace for President: Stand Up for America
   d) Our Time Has Come: Jesse Jackson '84

Your score: _____
Maximum base score: 45
Answers, page 169

Easy questions (1 point):

1) True or false: One of the signs gives the distance to Haiti.

2) Where are the signs located? That is, which place has a sign that indicates a distance of 0 km and 0 mi?

Medium questions (3 points):

3) What place is pointed to by the sign above Alaska's?

4) What place is 7305 km / 4539 mi away?

5) What place is pointed to by the bottom sign?

6) What color is the writing for the distances on the Kenia sign?

7) Two signs are light blue with white writing. Name both places pointed to by those signs.

Hard questions (5 points):

8) What color is the sign behind Portugal's that points in the opposite direction?

9) What is the furthest place? (And for 5 bonus points, how far away is it, in kilometers or miles?)

10) What sign has the same color scheme as Colombia's except that the colors of the places and the distances are swapped?

Your score: _____
Maximum base score: 37
Answers, page 169

Easy questions (1 point):

1) True or false: The blue T-shirt in the center of the photo reads "Italy."

2) How many people are wearing face paint, and where?

   a) one, on the left cheek
   b) one, on the right cheek
   c) two, on the same cheek
   d) two, on opposite cheeks

Medium questions (3 points):

3) For 3 points each, how many people are wearing:
   a) sunglasses?
   b) a hat?
   c) a bandana?

4) What color headphones are being worn by the woman on the right side of the photo?

5) For 3 points each, of the four women in the foreground:
   a) Which one is not raising one arm in a fist?
   b) Which one is wearing braces?
   c) Which one is not wearing earrings?

Hard questions (5 points):

6) What two countries are represented by the visible armbands in the photo?

7) One of the women who is raising her fist in the air is wearing a ring. What finger is it on?

8) From left to right, what are the main colors of the shirts worn by the four men whose faces are partly or mostly visible?

Your score: _____
Maximum base score: 38
Answers, page 170

64

Easy questions (1 point):

1) True or false: There are two pyramids to the left of the camel on the "Egypt" sticker.

2) What animal's silhouette appears in the maple leaf on the "Canada" sticker?

3) For 1 point each, are the following images facing left or right?

   a) the kangaroo on the "Australia" sticker
   b) the ship on the "Cruise Liner" sticker
   c) the plane on the "Fly With Us" sticker
   d) the camel on the "Egypt" sticker
   e) the silhouetted animal on the "Canada" sticker

Medium questions (3 points):

4) What are the two cities on the "Cruise Liner" sticker?

5) On how many stickers can the flag of the United Kingdom be seen?

6) What image appears on the sticker that is nearest the left edge of the suitcase?

7) How many statues appear on the suitcase?

Hard questions (5 points):

8) Seven cities, states, and countries with six-letter names are printed on the suitcase. Name all seven for 5 points. (If you can name six, give yourself 3 points. If you can name five, 1 point.)

9) Three stickers include the word "welcome." What locations do those three stickers advertise?

10) How many flags appear on the "World Traveler" sticker in the upper right?

11) On the "World Traveler" sticker, what country's flag is directly opposite the flag of China?

Your score: _____
Maximum base score: 39
Answers, page 170

Easy questions (1 point):

1) True or false: The gas tank is more than half full.

2) On which side of the car is a door open?

Medium questions (3 points):

3) What temperature is it outside?

4) How many illuminated icons are green?

5) How many illuminated icons are red?

6) What capital letter appears in the center of the display?

7) Which side of the car is the gas tank on?

Hard questions (5 points):

8) What is the number on the odometer readout?

9) What is the highest number on the speedometer?

10) What is the reading on the tachometer (to the nearest 50 rpm)?

11) What digits on the tachometer are "in the red"?

12) What four-letter word can you spell with the four letters on the leftmost and rightmost readouts?

Your score: _____
Maximum base score: 42
Answers, page 170

Easy questions (1 point):

1) True or false: The sharp ends of the straight pins are pointing down.

2) Three of the following four items are stored in the same compartment. Which is the odd one out?
   a) elastic
   b) scissors
   c) seam ripper
   d) measuring tape

Medium questions (3 points):

3) What two colors of thread are in the top center compartment?

4) The following items can all be found in the far left or the far right compartments. Correctly identify all of their locations for 3 points. (Give yourself 1 point for getting three correct.)
   a) pink thread
   b) packet of needles
   c) navy blue thread
   d) black buttons

5) What is in the compartment to the left of the safety pins?

6) How many snaps are nipple-side-down?

Hard questions (5 points):

7) How many straight pins are there?

8) One compartment contains the following six colors of thread: green, pink, orange, red, yellow, and white. Place them in order from top to bottom. (Give yourself 3 points if you get 4 out of 6 correct.)

9) What is the rightmost visible number on the measuring tape?

10) In the lower left compartment, one of the spools of thread is showing the cardboard spool through three diamond-shaped gaps in the thread. Which color of thread is it?

11) How many spools of thread are in the same compartment as the thimble?

Your score: _____
Maximum base score: 39
Answers, page 170

Easy questions (1 point):

1) True or false: None of the children are playing a stringed instrument.

2) What color is the strap on the rightmost instrument?

Medium questions (3 points):

3) How many feet are not touching the floor?

4) Two children are wearing red shirts. What instruments are they playing?

5) Five shelves in the back of the room contain plastic bins labeled with stars. What is the color of the top bin's star?

6) What color shirt is being worn by the child playing the maracas?

7) Two plastic cars on shelves in the back of the room are the same color. What color?

8) For 3 points each identify which child or children (number them 1 to 6 from left to right for convenience) are described by the following:
   a) wearing white sneakers
   b) hair in pigtails
   c) looking down
   d) one leg over the side of the chair

Hard questions (5 points):

9) What two images on the carpet are two of the children's feet resting on?

10) On top of a shelf in the back of the room is a stack of three plastic cylinders. What are their colors, from top to bottom?

11) One of the children is playing a multicolored xylophone. What color is the highest note on that instrument?

Your score: _____
Maximum base score: 44
Answers, page 170

Easy questions (1 point):

1) True or false: There are 16 books.

2) What fruit is at the top of the rightmost book, "Cooking"?

Medium questions (3 points):

3) What is the title of the tallest book?

4) What years are covered in the "World History" book?

5) How many electrons are circling the nucleus of the atom on the "Theoretical Physics" book?

6) What is the only author's name shown?

7) What color is the book "The Art of Success"?

8) What image is on the book "Environment: Essentials of Nature Protection"?

9) What is the subtitle of the book "Mechanics & Engineering"?
   a) "Basic Course"
   b) "Essentials"
   c) "Practical Course"
   d) "Practical Reference"

10) What book is an "Extended Edition"?

Hard questions (5 points):

11) What is the year on the book "Organic Chemistry"?

12) What is the title of the book whose subtitle is "Key to Satisfaction"?

13) What is the subtitle of the book "Digital Photography"?

14) What book is to the left of the dictionary?

15) What letters in the title "Modern Design" are underlined with a rainbow line?

Your score: _____
Maximum base score: 51
Answers, page 170

To Do

√ Clean Gutters
√ Paint Garage Door
√ Fix Screen Door
√ Mow Lawn
√ Laundry
√ Wash Car
√ Vacuum
√ Dry Cleaning
√ Bathe Dog

Easy questions (1 point):

1) True or false: The highest visible number on the measuring tape is 3.

2) True or false: The work glove on top is a right-handed glove.

3) True or false: The clippers are open.

Medium questions (3 points):

4) Which of the following items is not touching the whisk broom?
   a) work gloves
   b) rubber gloves
   c) to-do list
   d) paintbrush

5) How many clothespins are there?

6) How many pairs of nails are lying across each other in an X?

7) What color are the outer bristles of the scrubbing brush?

8) For 3 points each, supply the missing words in the following items on the to-do list:
   a) _____ garage
   b) Wash _____
   c) Fix _____ (two words)

Hard questions (5 points):

9) What two entries on the to-do list are single words?

10) Identify the four items closest to the four corners of the photo.

11) Only one item does not lie over one of the gaps between planks of wood on the table. (Consider a group of the same type of items as a single item.) Which one?

Your score: _____
Maximum base score: 39
Answers, page 170

Easy questions (1 point):

1) True or false: The store is closed on Sundays.

2) Which is not a sign?
   a) Cold coconut
   b) Milkshakes
   c) Pineapple smoothie
   d) Water & snacks

Medium questions (3 points):

3) What are the three special flavors?

4) What fruit shape is the blackboard for the special?

5) How many bananas are drawn on the back of the bench?

6) The words "Cash only" are written on a white shape that is a what?
   a) circle
   b) diamond
   c) octagon
   d) trapezoid

7) What word follows "Frosted" on the sign in the upper left?

8) What sign is to the left of the "Sun teas" sign?

Hard questions (5 points):

9) How many times does the word "Fruit" or "Fruits" appear on signs?

10) What word is written vertically on a sign?

Your score: _____
Maximum base score: 30
Answers, page 170

Easy questions (1 point):

1) True or false: The top ad on the left side of the scoreboard is for Goya.

2) What is the current score of the game?

3) For a point each, are the following things to the left or the right of the scoreboard?
   a) Lincoln/Mercury ad
   b) Sharp/Aquos ad
   c) a smokestack

Medium questions (3 points):

4) What team is in the lead?

5) What inning is it (and for an extra point, which half)?

6) In which corner of the Budweiser ad is the Major League Baseball logo?

7) For 3 points each, correctly answer the following questions about the current batter:
   a) What is his name?
   b) What is his uniform number?
   c) What is his batting average?
   d) In what inning was his previous at-bat?
   e) What was the result of that at-bat?

Hard questions (5 points):

8) Two ads are visible in the stands to the left of the scoreboard. What are they for?

9) On the left side of the scoreboard, how many X's are made by the girders of the structure?

10) How many hits have there been so far in the game?

11) Draw the logo for the Hospital for Special Surgery.

12) How many times can the word "Sharp" be seen (not counting the URL)?

13) What is the URL for Arpielle Equipment Co.?

Your score: _____
Maximum base score: 60
Answers, page 170

Easy questions (1 point):

1) True or false: The car parked in front of the general store has whitewall tires.

2) On which corner of the general store sign does it say "You are here!"?

Medium questions (3 points):

3) Which brand of soda is not advertised somewhere in the picture?
a) Dr Pepper
b) 7up
c) Royal Crown Cola
d) Pepsi

4) What is the name of the general store?

5) Two fanciful creatures appear on the various Mobiloil and Mobilgas signs. What are they?

6) There are multiple Route 66 signs in the picture, with various different wordings. For 3 points each, of the wordings below, which appear furthest left, furthest right, and uppermost in the picture?
a) Route 66
b) Route U.S. 66
c) Historic U.S. 66
d) Route US 66 National Historic Highway

Hard questions (5 points):

7) What four items does the general store feature on its sign? Wording must match exactly. (Give yourself 2 extra points if you can name them in order. If you can only name three of the four, give yourself 3 points.)

8) What brand of motor oils is advertised on the rightmost wooden pillar?

9) According to one of the signs, parking is allowed only for what kind of car?

10) How many other signs have the same shape and orientation as the large "Drink Coca-Cola" sign (but are not necessarily the same size)?

Your score: _____
Maximum base score: 42
Answers, page 171

Easy questions (1 point):

1) True or false: The six visible faces of the giant fuzzy dice are in ascending numerical order.

2) How much does it cost to play?

3) How many heads are there on the counter? (And for an extra point, how many can be seen to be wearing monocles?)

Medium questions (3 points):

4) How many large stuffed Nemo dolls are there?

5) Of the giant fuzzy dice, what number is visible on the front of the green one?

6) Of the prizes numbered 5 and 29:
   a) both are packaged in cardboard boxes
   b) one is packaged in cardboard boxes
   c) neither is packaged in cardboard boxes

7) How many musical notes are there on the "Winning Numbers" sign? (Remember that if two notes are connected by a beam, they are still two notes.)

8) What direction is the central head facing?
   a) forward
   b) to its left
   c) backward
   d) to its right

Hard questions (5 points):

9) What are the four numbers in the second row of "Winning Numbers"? (Give yourself 3 points if you correctly name three out of four.)

10) Two different Spider-Man toys are available as prizes. What are the numbers they are labeled with?

11) What are the prizes in the two compartments with signs reading "Every Player Wins a Prize"?

12) The types of stuffed animal on the top row are: white cat, red dragon, orange bear, pink dog, and blue dog. Ignoring the partially visible red dragon at the left side of the photo and the partially visible blue dog at the right side of the photo, list the ten animals on the top row in order from left to right. (Give yourself 3 points if you correctly name seven out of ten.)

Your score: _____
Maximum base score: 39
Answers, page 171

Easy questions (1 point):

1) True or false: The man is holding the mug of coffee in his right hand.

2) Which of the following items or images does not appear somewhere in the picture?
   a) scissors
   b) binder clip
   c) light bulb
   d) five-pointed star

Medium questions (3 points):

3) What three items are sitting on top of the pile of folders, notebooks, and papers?

4) What colors are the two paperclips at one end of the ruler?

5) How many colored squares are there in the lower right of the computer screen?

6) What two words are the biggest ones on the web page being viewed?

7) How many pencils are there in the glass pencil holder on the right side of the photo? (And for a bonus point, what color is the pencil pointing straight up toward the top of the photo?)

Hard questions (5 points):

8) What key is the man's forefinger resting on?

9) What colors are the leftmost and rightmost of the colored squares in the lower right of the computer screen?

10) Place the following items in order from left to right in the picture:
    a) mechanical pencil
    b) rubber band ball
    c) leather case
    d) green ceramic plate

11) What two words appear in gray rectangles in the lower left of the computer screen?

12) What inch number on the ruler is partially obscured by the corner of a notebook?

Your score: ___
Maximum base score: 43
Answers, page 171

Easy questions (1 point):

1) True or false: The bird is sitting atop the third column of airlines.

2) Who is the terminal named for?

Medium questions (3 points):

3) Match the first words to the last words to form names on the sign.
   a) EVA   x) Air
   b) Fiji   y) Airlines
   c) Japan z) Airways

4) What three airlines consist of just three all-capital letters?

5) How many airlines are listed in each of the four columns?

6) What is the only airline that consists of three words?

7) What are the first and last airlines listed?

Hard questions (5 points):

8) What is the only one-word airline in the second column?

9) What airline is to the right of Iberia Airlines?

10) What three airlines start with the letter S?

Your score: _____
Maximum base score: 32
Answers, page 171

THE WAR OF MUNITIONS

HOW GREAT BRITAIN HAS MOBILISED HER INDUSTRIES

WOMEN in INDUSTRY

HIGH EXPLOSIVES

NATIONAL ARSENALS

THE ARMY

THE NAVY

HEAVY GUNS

MACHINE GUNS

WAR WORKERS

TRAINING SCHOOLS

BOMBS

GUN AMMUNITION

NATIONAL PROJECTILE FACTORIES

Easy questions (1 point):

1) True or false: The man in the "War Workers" illustration is holding a tool in his right hand.

2) True or false: The two men in the "Training Schools" illustration are facing each other.

Medium questions (3 points):

3) For 3 points each, in the two lines of text above the illustrations:
   a) What word has a British spelling?
   b) What letter has two lines drawn beneath it?
   c) What are all the words that begin with "H"?

4) In the "Gun Ammunition" illustration, which of the three bullets is the smallest?

5) Of the twelve illustrations with titles, what is the only title that is a single word?

6) In the title "Women in Industry," which letter in the word "Industry" is smaller than the rest? (And for 2 bonus points, which letter is surrounded by the machine's belt?)

7) What word is handwritten in the upper right?

8) Of the two men nearest the viewer in the bottom center illustration, how many are wearing hats?

Hard questions (5 points):

9) What are the titles of the illustrations above and below "The Army"?

10) What three words appear above an illustration of a scale?

11) According to the illustration, what number of arsenals existed "before the war" and what number are "working today"?

12) How many small people are holding up the sailor in the illustration under "The Navy"?

Your score: _____
Maximum base score: 48
Answers, page 171

Easy questions (1 point):

1) True or false: The pump number (indicated in a blue circle) is 8.

2) For 1 point each, what are the prices per gallon of regular, plus, and super?

Medium questions (3 points):

3) What three words appear below each of the prices on top of the pump?

4) What is the total price shown for the latest transaction?

5) Which grade of gas was this transaction? (It is indicated by an arrow over the LCD price, but you can also determine it by dividing the total price by the gallons pumped.)

6) What four words are on the red sticker in the lower left?

7) What is the middle octane number of the three shown on the yellow buttons?

8) What percentage of ethanol does the gas contain?

9) On the LCD display on the left, what two words come before "or Insert Card"?

Hard questions (5 points):

10) How many diagrams feature nozzles?

11) Debit and credit purchases above what dollar value require reswiping your card?

12) The number keypad on the left has seven buttons to its right arranged in four rows, with each row a different color. From top to bottom, what are the colors of the rows?

13) In the instructions on the right, what instruction comes between "No Card Reader?" and "Dispense Fuel"?

Your score: _____
Maximum base score: 45
Answers, page 171

4 min.

Easy questions (1 point):

1) True or false: There are more 3-D "Hobbit" showings than 2-D .

2) On the main marquee, what is the line between "WELCOME TO YOUR" and "TICKETS ON SALE NOW FOR"?

Medium questions (3 points):

3) How many lights are lit in the ceiling above the marquee?

4) Three items are listed below the showtimes in neon. What are they? (And for 3 bonus points, match them to the colors blue, red, and yellow.)

5) What is the top movie listed on the left marquee?

6) What are the two 3-D movies listed on the left marquee?

7) What color is the neon border on the sign that says "SHOWTIMES"?

Hard questions (5 points):

8) What film has a 1:30 showtime?

9) How many banisters can be seen on the stairs?

10) What three times is "Big Hero 6" playing?

Your score: _____
Maximum base score: 35
Answers, page 171

Easy questions (1 point):

1) True or false: The man in the center is holding two discs in his left hand.

2) What two letters are on each of the women's shirts?

3) Around the edge of the board, the women's hair alternates between light and dark except in one instance. Which one appears twice in a row?

Medium questions (3 points):

4) What is the top line of text on the license plate that the spinner is pointing at?

5) How many people are there in the picture?

6) The two license plate numbers nearest the viewer are made up entirely of zeroes. What are the states on those license plates?

7) Besides the District of Columbia, what is the only state whose name is abbreviated around the edge of the board?

8) Are the shadows in the photo going to the left or the right?

9) The spinner is (roughly) pointing toward a triangular region along the edge of the board. What state is in that region?

Hard questions (5 points):

10) How many visible regions around the edge of the board are labeled "Dist. of Columbia"?

11) How many of the women are seen holding discs in their left hand?

12) What are the leftmost and rightmost states whose regions lie along the top edge of the board?

13) One license plate's number consists of the numbers 1 through 6 consecutively, though not in consecutive order. What is the state on that license plate? (And for 3 bonus points, what is the license plate number?)

14) One woman is looking directly at the camera. On what state is her disc?

Your score: _____
Maximum base score: 49
Answers, page 171

Easy questions (1 point):

1) True or false: The skeleton is holding an hourglass in its right hand.

2) True or false: Protective netting can be seen on the figures on either side of the clock.

3) What color is the background behind the word "Aurora"?

Medium questions (3 points):

4) On the outer dial, which two of the digits from 0 to 9 are written in a nontraditional way?

5) How many points are there on the small golden star at the end of one of the clock's hands?

6) What continent is oriented toward the top of the clock face?

7) What astrological sign is framed between the hands representing the sun and moon?
   a) ♋ (Pisces)
   b) ♊ (Gemini)
   c) ♉ (Taurus)
   d) ♌ (Leo)

8) Of the three men, which one's knees are visible?
   a) man playing a musical instrument
   b) man with a cane
   c) man holding a mirror

Hard questions (5 points):

9) Place the four figures in order from left to right:
   a) man holding a mirror
   b) man playing a musical instrument
   c) man with a cane
   d) skeleton

10) Above the clock face is a stone carving of a dog (seen as if from overhead). What number is it nearest to?

11) What two numbers are nearest the Roman numeral VII on the left side of the clock face?

Your score: _____
Maximum base score: 33
Answers, page 171

Easy questions (1 point):

1) True or false: There is a double yellow line on the track.

2) Which lane (top, middle, or bottom) does not have an Impala in it?

Medium questions (3 points):

3) Each of the two cars in the middle lane has a large three-letter word on its hood. What are those words?

4) What does Car 6 have in the spot where the car behind it has "Menards"?

5) What car number has Bass Pro Shops on its hood?

6) What large white word is on the hood of the car in last place?

7) The track wall has horizontal lines dividing it into how many rows?

8) What word appears below "Power Pak" on one of the cars?

Hard questions (5 points):

9) What three roof numbers are not red?

10) What two door numbers are red?

Your score: _____
Maximum base score: 30
Answers, page 172

Easy questions (1 point):

1) True or false: The time on the iPad is one minute later than the time on the iPhone.

2) What day of the week is shown in the Calendar app's icon?

Medium questions (3 points):

3) What two words are in the upper left corner of both the iPad and the iPhone?

4) What is the difference between the percentage battery charge on the iPhone and the percentage battery charge on the iPad?

5) Which of these apps is on the iPhone, and not on the iPad?
   a) FaceTime
   b) Game Center
   c) Newsstand
   d) Photo Booth
   e) Stocks

6) What interstate highway number is on the Maps icon?

7) What is the image on the Health icon on the iPhone?

8) What number is shown on the Mail icon on the iPad?

Hard questions (5 points):

9) What is the only app common to the rightmost column of both the iPad and the iPhone?

10) What app is above the Compass icon on the iPhone?

11) The upper-right icon on the iPad and the upper-right icon on the iPhone start with the same letter. What are those two apps?

Your score: _____
Maximum base score: 35
Answers, page 172

Easy questions (1 point):

1) True or false: The closing date for "King Charles III" is January 31.

2) Match the shows ("Sunny Afternoon," "Women on the Verge of a Nervous Breakdown," and "King Charles III") to their theaters:
a) Harold Pinter Theatre
b) Playhouse Theatre
c) Wyndham's Theatre

Medium questions (3 points):

3) On the "Sunny Afternoon" poster, what letters of "Afternoon" have shoes?

4) On the "Women on the Verge of a Nervous Breakdown" poster, which woman has glasses?
a) the one sitting down
b) the one with a leopard-skin coat
c) the one with a ponytail
d) the one with a red coat

5) What does the king have on his face on the "King Charles III" poster?

6) For 3 points each, complete these quotes:
a) "Attendance is _____ "
b) "I swear you'll get _____ " (two words)
c) "Play of the year. A _____ " (two words)
d) "The West End's new '_____'" (three words)
e) "Utterly _____ "

Hard questions (5 points):

7) What is the 11-digit phone number on the "King Charles III" poster?

8) For 5 points each, how many red stars and how many black stars are on the "Sunny Afternoon" poster? (Take credit if you are within one of the correct answer.)

9) The blurb below from the "Sunny Afternoon" poster has four adjectives in the blank. Name any three. (Give yourself 3 points if you can only name two of them.)
"A belter! _____ —It has everything the Kinks had."

10) Name both actors listed on the "Women on the Verge of a Nervous Breakdown" poster. (Give yourself 3 points if you can name only one.)

Your score: _____
Maximum base score: 51
Answers, page 172

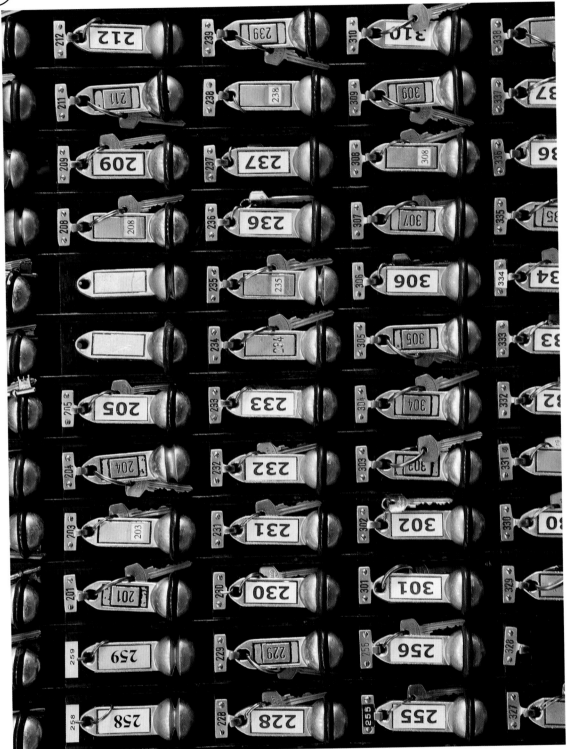

Easy questions (1 point):

1) True or false: The highest keyhook number shown is 338.

2) How many keyhooks are in each row?

Medium questions (3 points):

3) What keyhook number is printed in white on black tape?

4) What key is above #231?

5) What key is in the upper-left corner?

6) What keyhook number has nothing hanging from it?

7) In the top row, two unnumbered keyhooks separate two numbered keyhooks. What are those numbered keyhooks?

8) What key is to the left of #301?

Hard questions (5 points):

9) In the third row, what is the only key with its number written horizontally?

10) In the second row, two keyhooks have red around one screw. What is the number of either of these keyhooks? (Give yourself 2 bonus points if you can name both, but no points at all if you guess two numbers and both are not correct.)

11) Two keys are partially covering their room numbers. Which two? (Hint: They are both in the third row.)

Your score: _____
Maximum base score: 37
Answers, page 172

Easy questions (1 point):

1) One hand consists of three sevens. Are those sevens all red or all black? And for a bonus point, what color are the chips in the bet that accompanies that hand?

2) What is the total of the dealer's hand?

Medium questions (3 points):

3) One player has a blackjack (an ace plus a card valued at 10). What suit is that player's ace, and which card is the 10 (ten, jack, queen, or king)? (The suit of the card valued 10 is not needed, but take a bonus point if you can name it.)

4) How many columns of chips in the dealer's tray have red in them?

5) How many columns in the dealer's tray have red chips?

6) What is the total of the five-card hand?

Hard questions (5 points):

7) One player has two stacks of chips in the betting box. This is because the player "doubled down," meaning that the bet was doubled, and only one more card was dealt. That is why the third card is placed differently from other players' third cards. What is that card? And for a bonus point, what total did it give that player?

8) What card goes with the five of clubs and the three of hearts to make a hand? (To get credit, you must name both the rank and the suit.)

9) One particular rank of card can be seen as a club, a diamond, and a heart. What card rank is that?

10) One card rank is not seen anywhere in the image. What card rank is that?

Your score: _____
Maximum base score: 37
Answers, page 172

Easy questions (1 point):

1) True or false: The top letter in the eye chart is E.

2) True or false: The boy is wearing suspenders showing images of baseballs.

Medium questions (3 points):

3) How many lines does the eye chart have?

4) The letters in the fourth line in the eye chart can be rearranged to from a word. What word is that?
    a) COLT
    b) DOTE
    c) LOPE
    d) PLED

5) What letter is the boy pointing to?

6) What line is labeled 20/25?

7) Which of these correctly describes the boy?
    a) You can't see any of his teeth
    b) You can see some of his top teeth, but none of his bottom teeth
    c) You can see some of his bottom teeth, but none of his top teeth
    d) You can see some of his top teeth and some of his bottom teeth

8) The red bar separates what two lines in the eye chart?

Hard questions (5 points):

9) What letter is the last letter of four of the lines in the eye chart?

10) What are the letters in the second-to-last line of the eye chart, in order?

Your score: _____
Maximum base score: 30
Answers, page 172

Easy questions (1 point):

1) True or false: The London Underground ticket is a three-day pass.

2) What is the name of the MapGuide?

Medium questions (3 points):

3) What is the date (including the year) on the ticket?

4) A station is circled in pen on the right side of the London Underground map. Which train line is it on?
   a) red
   b) yellow
   c) green
   d) blue

5) Place these three theaters in order by their positions on the MapGuide from left to right: New Players, Noël Coward, Novello.

6) Place the same three theaters in order from top to bottom.

7) In the upper left corner of the ticket, one of the words of "London Underground" is cut off, forming a shorter word. What is the word?

8) How many black stripes are on the pen?

Hard questions (5 points):

9) What museum is seen on the MapGuide near the tip of the pen?

10) What two stations' names can be seen in full just below the bottom edge of the ticket? (Give yourself 2 points if you can name one of them.)

11) There are two theatres located in the upper left corner of the MapGuide. What are their names? (Give yourself 2 points if you can name one of them.)

12) Three of the four streets below meet at a single intersection on the MapGuide. Which is the odd one out?
    a) Bedford Street
    b) Floral Street
    c) Garrick Street
    d) King Street

13) Of the four London Underground stations listed below, two have connections to the National Rail (indicated by a ≥ logo). Which two?
    a) Limehouse
    b) Marble Arch
    c) Paddington
    d) Piccadilly Circus

Your score: _____
Maximum base score: 45
Answers, page 172

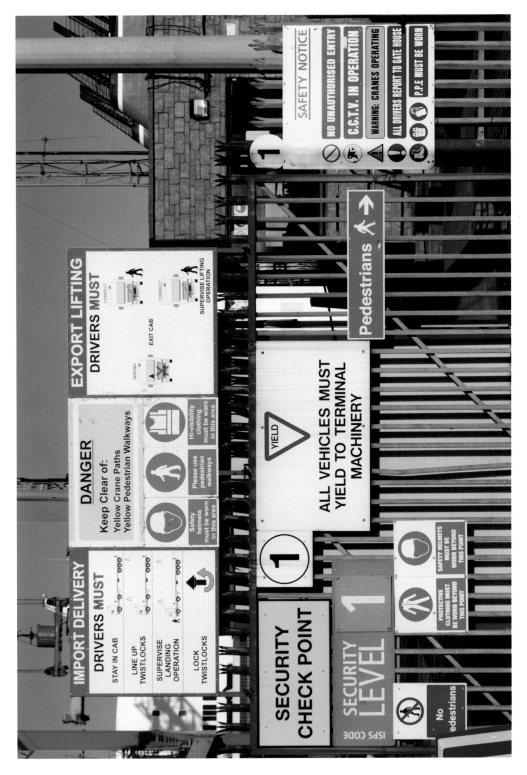

Easy questions (1 point):

1) True or false: This area is Security Level 1.

2) True or false: There is a bent pole behind the sign reading "Safety helmets must be worn beyond this point."

3) Which direction are pedestrians directed to walk?

Medium questions (3 points):

4) There are four things drivers must do for import delivery. Place them in the proper order:
   a) Line up twistlocks
   b) Lock twistlocks
   c) Supervise landing operation
   d) Stay in cab

5) For 3 points each, fill in the missing words in the following signs:
   a) All vehicles must yield to _____ (two words)
   b) _____ in operation
   c) All drivers report to _____ (two words)
   d) _____ clothing must be worn in this area
   e) Warning: _____ operating

Hard questions (5 points):

6) What three items of personal protective equipment appear to the left of the warning that reads "P.P.E. must be worn"?

7) What two things are you warned to "keep clear of" on a "Danger" sign?

8) How many exclamation points are there in total on all of the signs?

9) A "Yield" symbol appears above the word "vehicles" on one sign. Which two letters of "vehicles" is the "Yield" symbol's bottom point above, approximately?

10) Of all the human silhouettes depicted on the signs in profile, how many are facing the left side of the photo?

Your score: _____
Maximum base score: 46
Answers, page 172

112

Easy questions (1 point):

1) True or false: The face-up card in the center of the board is a Community Chest card.

2) To what color monopoly do the two deeds in the lower left corner of the picture belong?

   a) orange
   b) yellow
   c) green
   d) light blue

Medium questions (3 points):

3) What numbers are showing on the dice?

4) What is the value of the topmost bill in the center of the board?

5) In total, how many hotels are there on the board?

6) Of the deeds for the four railroads—B. & O., Pennsylvania, Reading, and Short Line—two are on the left side of the board and two are on the right. Which two are on the right?

7) Which two colors of monopoly do not have any houses or hotels built on them?

Hard questions (5 points):

8) For 5 points each, what spaces are the following pieces on?

   a) car
   b) thimble
   c) shoe
   d) hat

9) What is the five-word message on the face-up card in the center of the board?

10) Which two properties on the nearest edge of the board have two houses built on them? (And for 3 bonus points, what other two properties have two houses built on them?)

Your score: _____
Maximum base score: 50
Answers, page 172

✈ Departures

		Gate
19:35 Dusseldorf	Flight closing	A20
19:40 Frankfurt	Go to gate	A19
19:55 New York	Flight closing	B39
20:00 Nice	Go to gate	A6
20:00 Brussels	Boarding	A15
20:05 Johannesburg	Boarding	B43
20:10 Newcastle	Go to gate	A1
20:10 Stockholm	Go to gate	A18
20:15 Aberdeen	Go to gate	A2
20:15 Glasgow	Go to gate	A11
20:35 Dubai	Go to gate	B46
20:40 Manchester	Gate opens 19:50	
20:55 Hong Kong	Gate opens 19:40	
21:00 Edinburgh	Gate opens 20:10	
21:00 Riyadh		
21:25 M…		

22:30 Tel Aviv	Gate …
Flights for Friday, February 25th	
06:20 Istanbul	Gate o…
06:40 Manchester	Gate op…
06:45 Edinburgh	Gate open…
06:50 Geneva	Gate open…
06:55 Aberdeen	Gate ope…
06:55 Brussels	Gate open…
06:55 Copenhagen	Gate open…
07:00 Glasgow	Gate opens…
07:05 Prague	Gate open…
07:05 Munich	Gate opens…
07:05 Berlin	Gat…

Easy questions (1 point):

1) True or false: Six flights have the message "Go to gate."

2) What date is seen on the board?

Medium questions (3 points):

3) What destinations are currently boarding? (And for 3 bonus points, name either gate.)

4) What two-word phrase is shown in red in two places?

5) Three cities are listed for 07:05. Name two of them.

6) Which city is not scheduled for a time between 06:30 and 07:00?
   a) Edinburgh
   b) Geneva
   c) Istanbul
   d) Manchester

7) What destination city is also an adjective when its first letter is uncapitalized?

8) If you rotate the plane icon, what capital letter does it most closely resemble?

Hard questions (5 points):

9) What three destinations are two words?

10) What time does the gate open for the 20:40 flight to Manchester?

11) What are the scheduled times for the two flights to Glasgow?

12) What destination is listed below Stockholm?

13) What city is the plane at Gate B46 going to?

Your score: _____
Maximum base score: 48
Answers, page 173

Easy questions (1 point):

1) True or false: The cap of the ketchup bottle lying on the floor is closed.

2) For a point each, correctly identify the following details about the clock on the wall:
   a) the numbers the hour hand is between
   b) the numbers the minute hand is between
   c) the numbers the second hand is between

3) What is on the baby's head?

Medium questions (3 points):

4) Who in the picture is holding a handful of money (the mother, the daughter, the son, or the baby), and in which hand?

5) What colors are the two balloons?

6) Of the two photos on the wall, which one has been drawn on with markers, and which direction is it tilting?
   a) the left-hand photo, tilting left
   b) the left-hand photo, tilting right
   c) the right-hand photo, tilting left
   d) the right-hand photo, tilting right

7) One person in the picture is holding a cup. What color is it?

Hard questions (5 points):

8) How many gray and blue stripes are on each arm of the robot drawing on the wall?

9) Which of the following correctly describes the goldfish and duck?
   a) facing each other
   b) facing away from each other
   c) both facing the left side of the picture
   d) both facing the right side of the picture

10) Of the items listed below, select the two that are the furthest apart:
   a) lipstick
   b) basketball
   c) toast
   d) stack of books

11) Put the following items in order from left to right in the picture:
   a) robot picture drawn on a piece of paper
   b) scissors
   c) red suitcase
   d) paper bag

Your score: _____
Maximum base score: 37
Answers, page 173

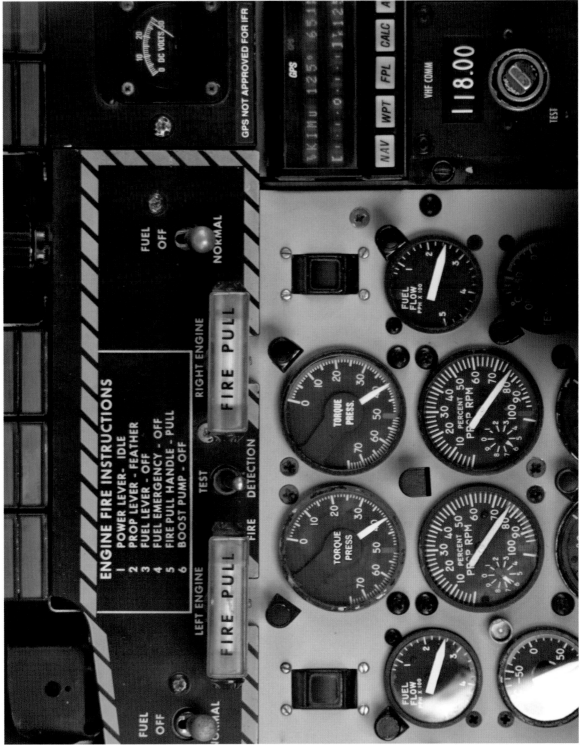

Easy questions (1 point):

1) True or false: The engine fire instructions have five steps.

2) What number is below "VHF COMM"?

Medium questions (3 points):

3) Provide the two abbreviations that complete this: "_____ not approved for _____"

4) What number on the torque press dials is marked with a red line?

5) On the toggle switch between the two fire pulls, what word is below the switch?

6) The fuel flow dials for both engines are pointing between what two numbers?

7) What four-letter word appears in the lower right corner above a small light?

Hard questions (5 points):

8) What do the two buttons between NAV and CALC say?

9) What is the second step of the engine fire instructions?

10) What is the highest number on the DC volts dial in the upper right?

Your score: _____
Maximum base score: 32
Answers, page 173

Easy questions (1 point):

1) True or false: The Post-It in the upper left reads (ignoring capitalization) "Don't worry! Be happy!"

2) Which of the following messages appears on one of the Post-Its?
   a) Remember to practice yoga
   b) Buy the milk
   c) Don't forget to feed the birds
   d) Write a to-do list

Medium questions (3 points):

3) How many Post-Its are there along the top edge of the screen?

4) Each of the following Post-Its' messages but one have a misspelled word. For 3 points each, indicate the way in which the word in question is misspelled (or if there is no misspelled word).
   a) Go to bank tomorrow
   b) Buy two tickets
   c) Meeting with Samantha Sunday
   d) Pick up dress from cleaner
   e) Urgent! Call!

5) How many Post-Its show a smiling face and nothing else?

Hard questions (5 points):

6) The following messages are each written on a different color of Post-It: green, lavender, orange, red, and yellow. Match all the messages to their correct colors for 5 points. (Give yourself 3 points if you match three out of the five messages.)
   a) Order the book
   b) Urgent! Meeting with Jacob
   c) Let's talk
   d) Call Mom!
   e) Just smile

7) How many Post-Its include a drawing of a heart? (And for an extra point, are those Post-Its all the same color or not?)

8) How many red Post-Its are there in total?

9) What message is written on the pink Post-It in the lower right corner?

Your score: _____
Maximum base score: 44
Answers, page 173

Easy questions (1 point):

1) True or false: The ball on top of the pole on the right side is green.

2) What URL is listed above the sign for "Wicked"?

Medium questions (3 points):

3) For 3 points each, match the shows to their quotes:
   a) "Jersey Boys" w) "The best West End musical for years"
   b) "Stomp" x) "An entertainment phenomenon"
   c) "War Horse" y) "Expect to be amazed"
   d) "Wicked" z) "London's 'best night out'"

4) The woman on the sidewalk to the right of the folding sign has which foot on the ground?

5) What two words are under the QR code on the folding sign?

6) For 3 points each, on which side of folding sign (left or right) are these listings?
   a) "Jeeves & Wooster"
   b) "Miss Saigon"
   c) The Tower of London
   d) "39 Steps"
   e) "Wicked"

7) Fill in the blank to complete the words on the "Lion King" sign: "Discover the _____ of London"

Hard questions (5 points):

8) What yellow items are displayed outside the store across the street by the phone booth?

9) What is listed under "EDF Energy London Eye" on the folding sign?

10) What show's poster is to the left of the "Jersey Boys" poster and above the "Stomp" poster?

Your score: _____
Maximum base score: 53
Answers, page 173

Easy questions (1 point):

1) True or false: The most common brand in the bin below the bottom shelf is Ziggy's.

2) What three-word phrase appears in the yellow area of the price labels?

Medium questions (3 points):

3) Arrange these Olivieri brand products from top to bottom (and for 3 bonus points, which one is a ravioli?):
   a) Beef
   b) Chicken & bacon
   c) Spinach & cheese

4) What is the largest word on the $4.79 packages on the right of the middle shelf?

5) On the bottom shelf, one product is upside down. What is its brand?

6) What is the weight of the $5 mortadella on the middle shelf?
   a) 200 g
   b) 250 g
   c) 2 × 175 g
   d) 2 × 225 g

Hard questions (5 points):

7) What is the lowest price on the top shelf?

8) What two words come before "Deli" in one of the brands?

9) What type of cheese is on the left of the bottom shelf, with a price of $2.99?

10) How many $5.00 labels are between the $2.99 and the $4.79 labels on the bottom shelf?

Your score: _____
Maximum base score: 37
Answers, page 173

EVACUATION PLAN

In case of FIRE use stairs unless otherwise instructed

1. Notify the inn operator (dial 0) or pull nearest fire alarm
2. If you hear the fire alarm, evacuate, don't try to investigate.
3. Proceed to nearest stairway and exit on the ground floor.
4. Be sure your door is cool before you open it.

5. If your door is hot, don't open it.
6. Crawl low under smoke.
7. If unable to exit your room:
   A. Close door and seal with wet towels.
   B. Stay near windows until help arrives.

● YOU ARE HERE
⊠ DO NOT USE ELEVATORS
▶ FIRE EXTINGUISHERS

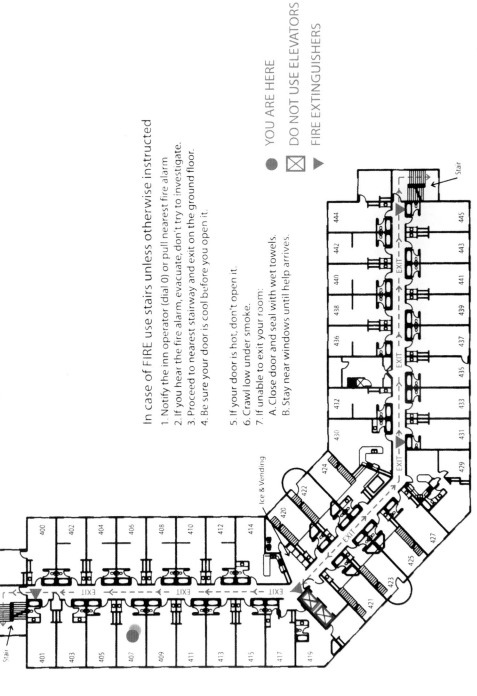

THANK YOU FOR STAYING WITH US. CHECK OUT TIME IS 12:00pm.

Easy questions (1 point):

1) True or false: Check out time is 1:00 pm.

2) True or false: The ice & vending machines are across the hall from the elevator.

3) True or false: All the red triangles on the floor plan are oriented identically.

4) How many numbered instructions are there?

Medium questions (3 points):

5) What room are you in, according to the red circle indicator?

6) Which two of the numbered instructions are separated by a blank line?

7) What room extends behind the elevators?

8) How many fire extinguishers are located on the floor?

9) For 3 points each, complete the following instructions:
   a) Notify the _____ (dial 0) or pull nearest fire alarm (two words)
   b) If you hear the fire alarm, evacuate, don't _____ (three words)
   c) Close door and _____ (four words)

Hard questions (5 points):

10) Which two rooms have balconies?

11) Which two rooms have a connecting doorway between them?

12) Of the words written in all capital letters, four begin with E. What are they?

13) The floor plan shows rooms from 400 to 445, but five numbers are not used. For 5 points, name any three of the unused numbers. (For 2 bonus points, name all five.)

Your score: _____
Maximum base score: 47
Answers, page 173

Easy questions (1 point):

1) True or false: The brand name of the jukebox is "Seaburg."

2) What is the last letter of the alphabet to appear on one of the jukebox buttons?

Medium questions (3 points):

3) The lettered jukebox buttons skip a letter. Which one?

4) Songs E7 and E8 are by the same artist. Who is it?

5) Songs F3 and F4 are by Dire Straits and Tears for Fears. In what color is each of their names printed?

6) Which of the following artists' names is typewritten rather than printed on its label?
   a) Gaio Padano
   b) E. Musiani
   c) Iva Zaniochi
   d) Riccardo Fogli

7) Which of the following songs is not found on the jukebox?
   a) "I'm on Fire"
   b) "Every Time You Go Away"
   c) "Slave to Love"
   d) "Dancing in the Street"

Hard questions (5 points):

8) Two labels are missing from the jukebox. What are the four corresponding letter/number codes for the empty slots?

9) What three artists are on the flip side of songs by Madonna? (Give yourself 3 points if you can name two of them.)

10) The two labels in the bottom row of the rightmost compartment of 10 labels contain the names of three dances. What are they? (Give yourself 3 points if you can name two of them.)

11) What artist performs the song "Occhi Blu"?

Your score: _____
Maximum base score: 37
Answers, page 173

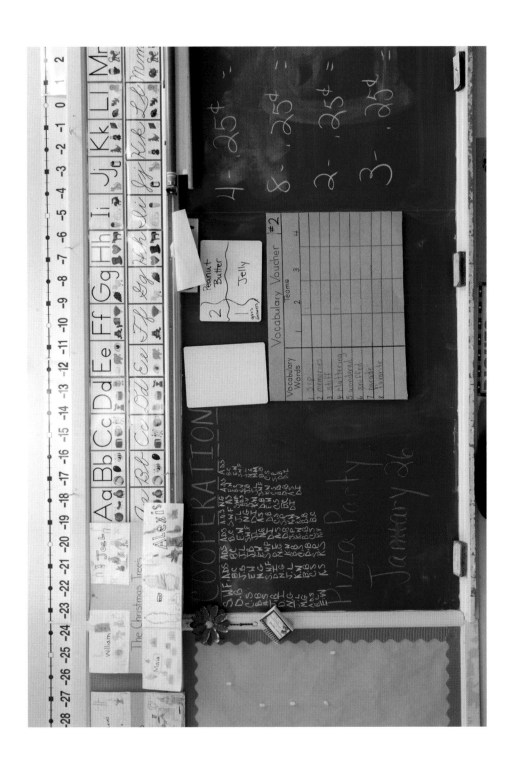

Easy questions (1 point):

1) True or false: There are three erasers on the chalkrail.

2) What is the date of the pizza party?

3) Which name does not appear on any of the Christmas tree drawings?
   a) Alexis
   b) Gordon
   c) Joel
   d) William

Medium questions (3 points):

4) What shape is above −9 on the number line?
   a) a solid square
   b) a solid circle
   c) an outlined square
   d) an outlined circle

5) What color is the trim around the yellow bulletin board?

6) Name two of the three objects on the "H" alphabet card. (Give yourself 2 bonus points if you can name all three).

7) How many white pushpins are visible on the yellow bulletin board?

Hard questions (5 points):

8) What are the initials that appear at the top of six of the eight columns under the word "Cooperation"?

9) From top to bottom, what are the four numbers that appear to the left of ".25¢" on the chalkboard?

10) What alphabet card is directly below the O on the number line?

11) What are the bottom two vocabulary words?

Your score: _____
Maximum base score: 37
Answers, page 173

134

Easy questions (1 point):

1) True or false: The sign "mwah" is written in all lowercase letters in script.

2) What shape is formed in the hole of the "O" in the sign "love" where the "L" and "O" are above the "V" and "E"?
   a) Africa
   b) a football
   c) a dollar sign
   d) a heart

Medium questions (3 points):

3) What word is below the script "mr & mrs" and to the left of the print "Mr & Mrs"?

4) What word from this sentence is not shown? "Friends welcome awesome romantic kisses."

5) Which one of these shapes is not shown?
   a) anchor
   b) New Jersey
   c) owl
   d) star

6) For 3 points each, fill in the blanks to complete the signs:
   a) Oh My _____
   b) Let's Be _____

7) What word is a palindrome?

Hard questions (5 points):

8) What word shown can be formed by removing the last three letters of another word shown?

9) What word has a bird perched on its first letter?

10) What word is in the bottom left corner?

11) What color is the outermost "chaos" sign?

Your score: _____
Maximum base score: 40
Answers, page 174

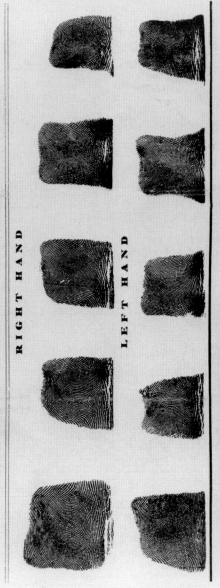

POLICE DEPARTMENT
CITY OF NEW YORK

CLASSIFICATION

CTIVE DIVISION
ULAR NO. 1
ARY 15, 1934

WANTED FOR VIOLATION OF

Federal Income Tax Law

PLEASE CLASSIFY AND FILE WITH YOUR FINGERPRINT RECORDS

RIGHT HAND

LEFT HAND

DESCRIPTION—Age 31 years; height 5 feet, 7 inches; weight 165 pounds; medium build; brown hair; gray eyes; fair complexion. B-50149.

Wanted by the Internal Revenue Service, United States Government, New York City. They hold warrant for indictment of the above charge.

Kindly search your Prison Records as this man may be serving a sentence for some minor offense.

If located, arrest and hold as a fugitive from justice, and advise Detecive Division, by wire.

JOHN F. O'RYAN,
Police Commissioner

TELEPHONE SPring 7-3100

ARTHUR FLEGENHEIMER

ALIASES DUTCH SCHULTZ, ARTHUR SCHULTZ, GEORGE SCHULTZ, JOSEPH HARMON AND CHARLES HARMON

Easy questions (1 point):

1) True or false: The fingerprints of the left hand are above the fingerprints of the right hand.

2) In the profile mug shot, which side of the suspect's face can be seen?

Medium questions (3 points):

3) What is the suspect's name?

4) What two surnames does the suspect use in his aliases?

5) What year is shown in the upper-left corner?

6) The suspected is wanted for violation of what? (Your answer must match the four-word answer exactly.)

7) What is the phone number at the bottom?

8) What is the suspect's age?

Hard questions (5 points):

9) What is the suspect's height and weight?

10) What is the suspect's hair and eye color?

11) What is the police commissioner's middle initial?

12) What five-digit number follows the "B" in the suspect's identification number?

Your score: _____
Maximum base score: 40
Answers, page 174

Easy questions (1 point):

1) True or false: One magnet is in the shape of a right flip-flop.

2) What image is on the Washington, D.C., magnet?
   a) Jefferson Memorial
   b) Lincoln Memorial
   c) Washington Monument
   d) White House

Medium questions (3 points):

3) How many orcas are on the magnet for MarineLand Canada?

4) A thermometer is on a magnet from where?

5) What animal appears on the magnet for African Lion Safari? (Hint: It's not a lion.)

6) The name of what place appears below "Welcome to the wilderness" on a magnet shaped like a lantern?

7) What color is the penguin's hat on the North Pole magnet?

8) What landmark is on the magnet between the Empire State Building magnet in the upper-left corner and the "I♥NY" T-shirt magnet?

9) What shape is the NASA magnet?

Hard questions (5 points):

10) What magnet is to the left of the Epcot magnet?

11) Four names are written on the magnet in the lower-left corner. For 5 points, name all four. (Give yourself 3 points if you can name three of them.)

12) What two playing cards are on the Atlantic City magnet?

13) Where is the Martyrs' Shrine magnet from?

Your score: _____
Maximum base score: 43
Answers, page 174

Nutrition Facts (1)

Nutrition Facts
Serving Size 1 Box (27g)

Amount Per Serving

Calories 100 Calories from Fat 0

	% Daily Value*
Total Fat 0g	0%
Saturated Fat 0g	0%
Trans Fat 0g	
Cholesterol 0mg	0%
Sodium 95mg	4%
Total Carbohydrate 24g	8%
Dietary Fiber 2g	9%
Sugars 8g	
Protein 1g	

Vitamin A	0%	•	Vitamin C	8%
Calcium	0%	•	Iron	8%
Vitamin D	8%	•	Thiamin	20%
Riboflavin	20%	•	Niacin	20%
Vitamin B6	20%	•	Folic Acid	20%
Vitamin B12	20%	•	Zinc	8%

* Percent Daily Values are based on a 2,000 calorie diet. Your daily values may be higher or lower depending on your calorie needs:

		Calories	2,000	2,500
Total Fat	Less than		65g	80g
Sat. Fat	Less than		20g	25g
Cholesterol	Less than		300mg	300mg
Sodium	Less than		2,400mg	2,400mg
Total Carbohydrate			300g	375g
Dietary Fiber			25g	30g

Nutrition Facts (2)

Nutrition Facts
Serving Size 1 Box (39g)

Amount Per Serving

Calories 150 Calories from Fat 10

	% Daily Value*
Total Fat 1g	2%
Saturated Fat 1g	5%
Trans Fat 0g	
Cholesterol 0mg	0%
Sodium 170mg	7%
Total Carbohydrate 34g	11%
Dietary Fiber less than 1g	2%
Sugars 15g	
Protein 2g	

Vitamin A	30%	•	Vitamin C	30%
Calcium	4%	•	Iron	30%
Vitamin D	15%	•	Vitamin E	30%
Thiamin	30%	•	Riboflavin	30%
Niacin	30%	•	Vitamin B6	30%
Folic Acid	30%	•	Vitamin B12	30%
Zinc	10%			

* Percent Daily Values are based on a 2,000 calorie diet. Your daily values may be higher or lower depending on your calorie needs:

		Calories	2,000	2,500
Total Fat	Less than		65g	80g
Sat. Fat	Less than		20g	25g
Cholesterol	Less than		300mg	300mg
Sodium	Less than		2,400mg	2,400mg
Total Carbohydrate			300g	375g
Dietary Fiber			25g	30g

Nutrition Facts (3)

Nutrition Facts
Serving Size 1 Box (27g)

Amount Per Serving

Calories 100 Calories from Fat 10

	% Daily Value*
Total Fat 1g	2%
Saturated Fat 0.5g	3%
Trans Fat 0g	
Cholesterol 0mg	0%
Sodium 125mg	5%
Total Carbohydrate 24g	8%
Dietary Fiber 3g	10%
Sugars 12g	
Protein 1g	

Vitamin A	8%	•	Vitamin C	20%
Calcium	0%	•	Iron	20%
Vitamin D	8%	•	Thiamin	20%
Riboflavin	20%	•	Niacin	20%
Vitamin B6	20%	•	Folic Acid	20%
Vitamin B12	20%	•	Zinc	8%

* Percent Daily Values are based on a 2,000 calorie diet. Your daily values may be higher or lower depending on your calorie needs:

		Calories	2,000	2,500
Total Fat	Less than		65g	80g
Sat. Fat	Less than		20g	25g
Cholesterol	Less than		300mg	300mg
Sodium	Less than		2,400mg	2,400mg
Total Carbohydrate			300g	375g
Dietary Fiber			25g	30g

Nutrition Facts (4)

Nutrition Facts
Serving Size 1 Box (34g)

Amount Per Serving

Calories 130 Calories from Fat 0

	% Daily Value*
Total Fat 0g	0%
Saturated Fat 0g	0%
Trans Fat 0g	
Cholesterol 0mg	0%
Sodium 170mg	7%
Total Carbohydrate 30g	10%
Dietary Fiber less than 1g	3%
Sugars 12g	
Protein 2g	

Vitamin A	10%	•	Vitamin C	10%
Calcium	0%	•	Iron	25%
Vitamin D	10%	•	Thiamin	25%
Riboflavin	25%	•	Niacin	25%
Vitamin B6	25%	•	Folic Acid	25%
Vitamin B12	25%			

* Percent Daily Values are based on a 2,000 calorie diet. Your daily values may be higher or lower depending on your calorie needs:

		Calories	2,000	2,500
Total Fat	Less than		65g	80g
Sat. Fat	Less than		20g	25g
Cholesterol	Less than		300mg	300mg
Sodium	Less than		2,400mg	2,400mg
Total Carbohydrate			300g	375g
Dietary Fiber			25g	30g

Easy questions (1 point):

1) True or false: All four boxes have 0mg of cholesterol.

2) Place the box colors (black, blue, green, and yellow) in order from left to right.

Medium questions (3 points):

3) Which isn't a box weight?
   a) 27g
   b) 34g
   c) 37g
   d) 39g

4) How many of the boxes have less than 25% of the daily value of vitamin C?

5) What three words appear on the line above the calories on all four boxes?

6) What is on the line below sugars?

7) What vitamin appears on only one box? For a bonus point, what color box is it on? And for 2 additional points, what percentage of the daily value is it?

8) How many milligrams of sodium are in the box with the lowest sodium per serving?

Hard questions (5 points):

9) How many additional grams of saturated fat are in the daily 2,500-calorie diet than in the 2,000-calorie diet?

10) What is the total number of calories per single serving in all four boxes?

11) What word is italicized on all the boxes?

Your score: _____
Maximum base score: 38
Answers, page 174

Easy questions (1 point):

1) True or false: The yellow cartridge missing its label has "Pokemon" written on it.

2) Which of the following games appears more than once in the photo?
   a) Navy Seals
   b) Gex 3
   c) The Addams Family
   d) Turrican

Medium questions (3 points):

3) The names of two games on black cartridges are visible. What are they?

4) One game has someone's name written on it in marker. What is the name? (And for 2 bonus points, what is the game?)

5) What is the subtitle of the Teenage Mutant Ninja Turtles game?

6) For 3 points each, provide the missing words in the following game titles:
   a) Motocross _____
   b) Kirby's _____
   c) GB RPG _____ in 1
   d) Die _____

Hard questions (5 points):

7) Two games with six-letter titles share all of the letters in their names except for the middle two letters. Which games? (Hint: They are in the same row.)

8) What game lies diagonally between Golf and Tom and Jerry?

9) What game appears to the right of the game whose label is torn partly off?

Your score: _____
Maximum base score: 40
Answers, page 174

Easy questions (1 point):

1) True or false: On the ticket with the tic-tac-toe board, the center square is a heart.

2) What color is the dragon that appears on two tickets?

Medium questions (3 points):

3) How much is the $250 Million Cash Spectacular ticket?

4) How many chances to win are there on the Set for Life ticket?

5) What is the top prize on the Lucky Green ticket?

6) What are the three initial letters of the game on the $2 ticket between the $250 Million Cash Spectacular and the Set for Life tickets?

7) What are the four winning numbers on the Set for Life ticket?

Hard questions (5 points):

8) What symbol is revealed in the upper left scratch-off of the upper left ticket?

9) Fill in the blank from the $250 Million Cash Spectacular ticket:
"Over _____ prizes from $100 to $1 million!"

10) What is the URL for the 2nd Chance Draw?

11) Name any three numbers from the bottom row of six prize numbers on the Set for Life ticket.

Your score: _____
Maximum base score: 37
Answers, page 174

Easy questions (1 point):

1) True or false: Three people can be seen in the photo on the Empire State Building's ad card.

2) What name goes in the blank: "_____ is Back!"

3) What network has an ad for its studio tour?
   a) ABC
   b) CBS
   c) Fox
   d) NBC

Medium questions (3 points):

4) Where is the flea market with "up to 170 vendors"?

5) What show's ad card boasts that it won the 2008 Tony Award for Best Musical?

6) What word in yellow shares the "In" of "Intrepid" on its ad card?

7) According to its card, "Tonight belongs to" what show?

8) On the right, one slot has two of its cards sticking out crookedly. What is it for?

Hard questions (5 points):

9) What store's ad card is between the ones for "Chicago" and "Bye Bye Birdie"?

10) For 5 points each, fill in the blanks:
    a) "Fuerza Bruta: _____" (two words)
    b) _____ Freestyle
    c) Titanic: The _____ Exhibition

Your score: _____
Maximum base score: 38
Answers, page 174

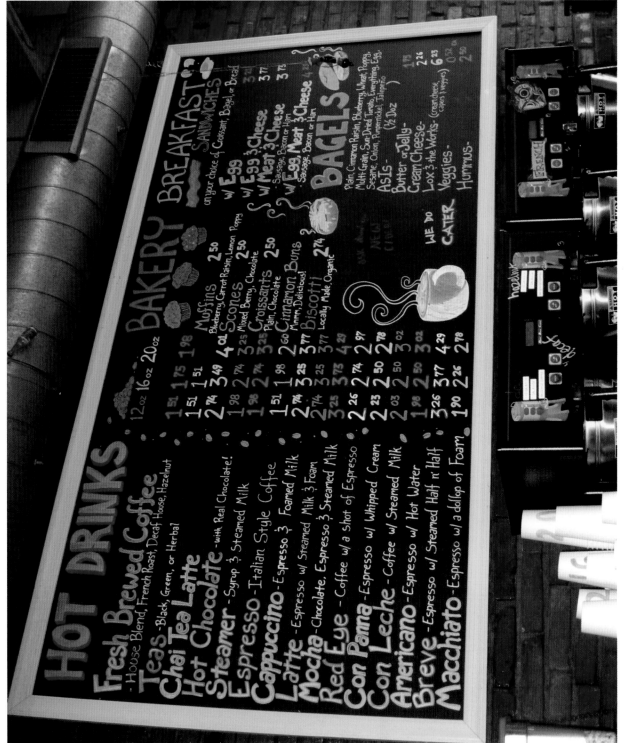

Easy questions (1 point):

1) True or false: The largest available size of coffee is 24 ounces.

2) Which of the following flavors of bagel does not appear on the menu?
   a) Multi-Grain
   b) Blueberry
   c) Asiago Cheese
   d) Sun-Dried Tomato

Medium questions (3 points):

3) A cut-out picture of what animal is taped to one of the coffee machines?

4) According to the menu, a macchiato is served with what amount of foam?

5) What coffee item on the menu contains syrup?

6) How many drawings of muffins appear on the menu?

7) What menu item is described as "Mmmm, delicious!"?

Hard questions (5 points):

8) What are the two available flavors of scones?

9) What is "the works" on a bagel?

10) How much does a cup of tea cost?

11) How many coffee drinks on the menu end with "O"?

12) Place the four available types of coffee in order from left to right, as they are indicated on the machines at the bottom of the photo:
    a) House Blend (unlabeled)
    b) Decaf House
    c) French Roast
    d) Hazelnut

Your score: _____
Maximum base score: 42
Answers, page 174

Easy questions (1 point):

1) True or false: There is a sticker on the hubcap of the car.

2) Which of these branches of the U.S. military is represented by more than one sticker on the car?
   a) Air Force
   b) Army
   c) Marines
   d) Navy

Medium questions (3 points):

3) For 3 points each, fill in the blanks of the following stickers:
   a) _____ under car (two words)
   b) Caution: future _____ inside
   c) _____ Motorcycle Speedway
   d) Working is for people who don't know how to _____ !!!
   e) _____ Hawaiian Island
   f) Bikers are tired of being injured ... for America's right to _____ (two words)

4) What is the phone number to report drug smuggling to U.S. customs?

5) What sports team's logo can be seen on the trunk of the car?

Hard questions (5 points):

6) What is the frequency of the radio station KLOS?

7) On the sticker that reads, "Gotcha, No Brains No Headache," how many figures are there, and what color is their hair?

8) What does the sticker above "Spoiled Rotten" read?

Your score: _____
Maximum base score: 41
Answers, page 174

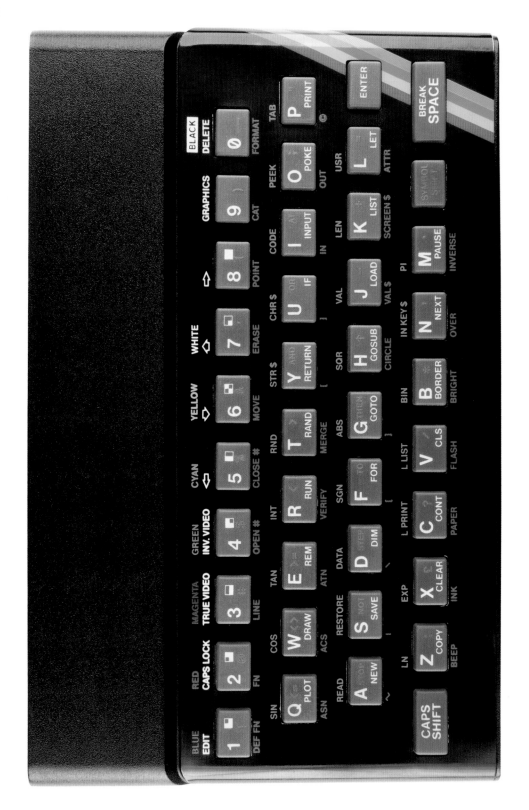

Easy questions (1 point):

1) True or false: The color listed above the "3" button is magenta.

2) How many colors are in the rainbow design?

Medium questions (3 points):

3) What two words are on the lower-right button?

4) How many buttons are in the row starting with "A"?

5) What word is on the "Z" button?

6) What word in red is to the left of the word "Merge"?

7) "Cat" is below what number?

8) What letter's button has green, white, and red words that all start with that letter? (And for 2 bonus points each, name any of them.)

Hard questions (5 points):

9) What four-letter green word becomes a new word when reversed?

10) What is the only eight-letter word shown?

11) What two words are on the "D" button?

Your score: _____
Maximum base score: 41
Answers, page 175

Easy questions (1 point):

1) True or false: Every book on the top shelf has a sticker on it.

2) Which of the following celebrities cannot be seen in the photo?
   a) Martin Short
   b) Gordie Howe
   c) Hillary Clinton
   d) Mindy Kaling

Medium questions (3 points):

3) Two books on the top shelf have shoes on their covers. Which books?

4) Who is the employee whose "pick" multiple books on the shelves are?

5) For 3 points each, fill in the blanks of the following book titles:
   a) "The Opposite of _____"
   b) "The Weight of _____"
   c) "The Map of _____"
   d) "The Back of _____" (two words)

6) One title appears on two different shelves with two different covers. Which?

Hard questions (5 points):

7) How much does the book about Leonard Cohen cost?

8) Of the fully visible books on the second shelf, how many adjacent ones have a "Spotlight" sticker?

9) The last name of one author is the same as an adjacent author's first name. What is the name they have in common?

10) What color is the border of the cover of Maya Angelou's "Rainbow in the Cloud"?

11) What two alliterative two-word phrases appear in the title of the book whose cover depicts two bowls being held?

Your score: _____
Maximum base score: 48
Answers, page 175

156

Easy questions (1 point):

1) True or false: The Zambia coin is from the 1990s.

2) Juan Carlos I is facing which way?
   a) up
   b) down
   c) left
   d) right

Medium questions (3 points):

3) What country is the coin with a gull and setting sun from? (Just the first seven letters are visible, so that's all you need to get credit.)

4) What word appears at the top of the coin that says "Singapore"?

5) How many coins have visible holes?

6) What is the denomination of the coin with a crescent, a flower, and a single star?

7) Elizabeth II is on a coin from where?

8) Two coins say "Koningin der Nederlanden" on them and are preceded by a name. For 3 points each, what are those names?

Hard questions (5 points):

9) Place these coins from top to bottom:
   a) Bahrain
   b) Brasil
   c) Estados Unidos Mexicanos
   d) Hong Kong

10) What are the initials on the Canadian coin that says "Pride" and "Fierté"?

11) A gold-and-silver coin in the lower right that depicts a garuda (an eaglelike creature) with a heraldic shield on its chest is from what year?

Your score: _____
Maximum base score: 38
Answers, page 175

CAL STATE NORTHRIDGE
KCSN BENEFIT PRESENTS
TOM PETTY
& THE HEARTBREAKERS
PLAZA DEL SOL PERF HALL
SAT OCT 29 2011 7:30 PM

NEDERLANDER PRESENTS
DON HENLEY
W/ SPECIAL GUEST
THE GREEK THEATRE
RAIN OR SHINE/4.75 FF
SAT SEP 17 2011 7:30PM

NEDERLANDER PRESENTS
EVENING W/ PETER FRAMPTON
FCA 35 TOUR
THE GREEK THEATRE
RAIN OR SHINE/4.75 FF
SAT JUL 30 2011 7:30PM

AN EVENING WITH
JASON BONHAM'S
LED ZEPPELIN EXPERIENCE
THE GREEK THEATRE
RAIN OR SHINE/4.75 FF
FRI MAY 27 2011 8:00PM

AEG LIVE PRESENTS
MARK&BRIAN CHRISTMAS SHOW
FEAT. STEVE MILLER BAND
NOKIA THEATRE L.A. LIVE
777 CHICK HEARN CT, LA
THU DEC 15 2011 7:30 PM

AEG LIVE WELCOMES
BON JOVI
THE CIRCLE TOUR
WWW.BONJOVI.COM
STAPLES CENTER
THU MAR 04 2010 7:30PM

AN EVENING WITH
RUSH
TIME MACHINE TOUR
GIBSON AMPHITHEATRE
NO CAMERAS OR RECORDERS
WED AUG 11, 2010 7:30PM

LIVE NATION PRESENTS
IRON MAIDEN
WWW.IRONMAIDEN.COM
VERIZON AMPHITHEATER
RAIN OR SHINE
THU AUG 09 2012 7:30 PM

LIVE NATION PRESENTS
JOURNEY
THE ECLIPSE TOUR
VERIZON AMPHITHEATER
WWW.JOURNEYMUSIC.COM
SAT JULY 23 2011 7PM

VAN HALEN
WWW.VAN-HALEN.COM
KOOL & THE GANG
STAPLES CENTER
LOS ANGELES, CA
FRI JUN 01 2012 7:30PM

Easy questions (1 point):

1) True or false: No ticket is for Sunday, Monday, or Tuesday.

2) What is the venue for the three green tickets?

Medium questions (3 points):

3) How many tickets have a start time other than 7:30 P.M.?

4) Who is the performer on the Cal State Northridge ticket?

5) For 3 points each, name the tours mentioned on these bands' tickets:
   a) Bon Jovi
   b) Journey
   c) Rush

6) The Evening W/ Peter Frampton ticket is located where among the ten tickets?

7) The backgrounds of three tickets on the left give what URL?

8) What show had a $125 base ticket price?

Hard questions (5 points):

9) The ticket whose seat is #141 is for what row?

10) What two bands are on the lower left ticket?

11) Which of these is not a number above a bar code?
   a) 184183294550
   b) 496993905456
   c) 71846553761
   d) 93252186l009

Your score: _____
Maximum base score: 41
Answers, page 175

Easy questions (1 point):

1) For 1 point each, are the posters for the following shows on the left side of the photo or the right side of the photo?
   a) "The Addams Family"
   b) "Avenue Q"
   c) "Billy Elliot"
   d) "Wicked"

2) What days "are a drag," according to a poster featuring RuPaul?

Medium questions (3 points):

3) On the left side of the photo, what two digits are visible on the side of the ticker that is facing you?

4) What word appears on a green background on the top screen in the center of the photo?

5) Three bank logos appear somewhere in the photo. Give yourself 3 points for each one that you can name.

6) On the right side of the photo, four advertisements for musicals appear in a 2-by-2 array. What show's poster appears diagonally opposite "Phantom of the Opera"?

Hard questions (5 points):

7) What basketball player appears on an ad?

8) In the center of the photo, how many pieces is the image of the Coca-Cola can broken into?

9) A screen features a word game with letters in colored circles. How many green circles are there?

10) Fill in the blank with the correct year: "Wembley Stadium, London _____?"

6 min.

MATCH No/TEE TIME	PLAYER	PAR	1	2	3	4	5	6	7	8	9	OUT	10	11	12	13	14	15	16	17	18	IN	TOTAL	1	2	3
			4	4	3	4	4	4	5	3		36				4	3	5	3	5	4	4	35	71			
22	CLARKE D	-10	4	3	4	3	4	4	5	3		33			4	4	2							68	70	69
	PARK D	-6	4	3	4	4	4	5	3	5		35			5	4	3							72	67	68
23	GONZALEZ R	-6	4	3	4	4	5	4	5	3		36			4	4	3							69	70	68
	VIBE-HASTRUP M	-8	4	4	3	5	4	4	5	3		35			4	3	3							69	71	67
24	McLARDY A	-9	4	4	3	4	3	4	5	3		34			4	4								66	68	72
	ERLANDSSON M	-10	4	3	3	4	3	4	5	3		33			4	4								69	66	71
25	DIXON D	-9	4	4	3	4	4	4	5	3		34			4	4								68	68	70
	KAMTE J	-10	4	4	3	4	4	3	5	3		34			3	4								65	72	69
26	WALL A	-8	3	4	3	4	4	4	5	3		35												69	70	67
	LARSEN JA	-8	4	5	3	5	4	5	2	3		35												68	72	66
27	JONZON M	-6	5	4	3	4	4	4	5	6														64	70	71
	EDFORS J	-10	4	4	3	4	3	4	4	5														68	68	69

Easy questions (1 point):

1) True or false: No golfer shot a 6 or higher on any hole.

2) What is par for the course (the yellow number under "Total")?

Medium questions (3 points):

3) Who has the only eagle (two under par, indicated by a red number on a yellow background)? And for a bonus point, what hole was it on?

4) What two players playing as a twosome have last names that rhyme?

5) What does it say in the top left corner to the left of "Player"?

6) What is Vibe-Hastrup's first initial?

7) What is par for the 16th hole?

8) What number is to the left of McLardy's name?

Hard questions (5 points):

9) What player shot a 4 on the 8th hole?

10) Who shot the lowest round (the lowest number under "1," "2," or "3" on the right)? And for a bonus point, what was the score of that low round?

11) Who is Wall playing with?

12) What player has exactly two birdies (indicated by red numbers) and two bogeys (indicated by light blue numbers) on the first nine holes?

Your score: _____
Maximum base score: 42
Answers, page 175

Easy questions (1 point):

1) Is the brand of the product on the right of the top shelf Aunt Jemima or Uncle Ben's?

2) Which Campbell's soup isn't seen?
   a) Chicken noodle
   b) Cream of chicken
   c) Old fashioned tomato rice
   d) Tomato noodle

Medium questions (3 points):

3) What is the brand of organic sauce on the top shelf?

4) To the right of the Hershey syrup on the middle shelf is an upside-down can of Campbell's soup. What kind of soup is it?

5) On the right of the middle shelf is a box of instant mix for what beverage?

6) What kinds of nuts are in most of the bags on the right side of the bottom shelf?

7) For 3 points each, on which shelf (top, middle, or bottom) are each of the following?
   a) black pepper
   b) Bush's chili beans
   c) Del Monte fresh cut whole kernel corn
   d) Hunt's mushroom pasta sauce
   e) Lipton onion soup mix
   f) Swanson beef broth

Hard questions (5 points):

8) What word is below "Progresso" and above "Roasted Chicken Rotini" on that can's label?

9) What words appear on the same line as a state outline on the can of Wolf brand chili (no beans)?

10) How many cans on the middle shelf are stacked on top of other cans?

Your score: _____
Maximum base score: 47
Answers, page 175

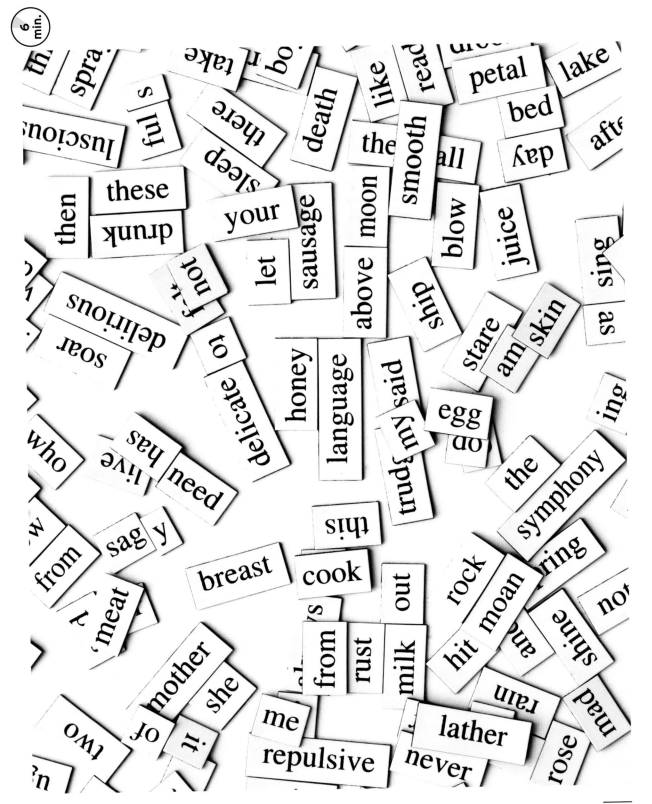

Easy questions (1 point):

1) True or false: The "sleep" and "bed" magnets are abutting.

2) Which of these magnets is not in the picture?
   a) "bacon"
   b) "egg"
   c) "juice"
   d) "milk"
   e) "sausage"

Medium questions (3 points):

3) The "y" magnet is to the right of what word?

4) What three-letter word appears on the magnet that's closest to the upper-left corner without being cut off by the edge of the picture?

5) What word is below the "honey" magnet?

6) The "me" magnet is partially covering a magnet with what nine-letter word?

7) What two-letter word is atop the "trudge" and "said" magnets?

Hard questions (5 points):

8) The "ship" magnet is abutting three other magnets. Name two of them.

9) What is the only word shown with two y's?

10) Place these four magnets in order from left to right:
    a) "breast"
    b) "death"
    c) "delirious"
    d) "lather"

Your score: _____
Maximum base score: 32
Answers, page 175

PAGES 7-8

1) True
2) False
3) 11:49
4) Norway
5) Russia
6) 3
7) 3; Canada, Japan, Switzerland
8) a) CNY; b) AUD; c) MXP; d) EUR
9) Switzerland (CHF), United Kingdom (GBP)
10) Norway, Russia

PAGES 9-10

1) True
2) True
3) The Adventuredome; 25
4) O; hotel
5) 3
6) Green, purple
7) a) Tatuado; b) world-class
8) d) triangle
9) b) wearing sunglasses, holding a drink in his left hand
10) 8
11) T, K, T
12) The Steak House

PAGES 11-12

1) False (Benjamin Franklin was not president)
2) b) James (Garfield and Monroe)
3) Lincoln Memorial; 1 dollar
4) Washington; 10 cents (lower left stamp, although unlabeled, depicts Washington with the same portrait as the red 2-cent stamp)
5) Far right of the middle row
6) (Woodrow) Wilson
7) (Benjamin) Franklin
8) NY (New York)
9) Garfield, Cleveland (on the postmark)
10) Lincoln, Washington
11) The middle row; 10 cents
12) U.S. Postage; lower left
13) 27 cents

PAGES 13-14

1) True
2) False
3) "Eat these every day"
4) b) in a diagonal line
5) 8; milk and meat, bread and butter
6) 5
7) Milk, egg carton (take credit for "eggs")
8) Peas
9) Cabbage
10) "3 or 4"
11) 6
12) d, b, a, c

PAGES 15-16

1) True
2) 09 (take credit for "lower left")
3) 16 and 22
4) "Using conditions"; 17
5) 3
6) a) Kindly use; b) left-end; c) information
7) 13
8) 16, 20, 23
9) 6
10) 22

PAGES 17-18

1) False
2) 250
3) Sweets
4) Kate Upton
5) $2.49
6) Big Red
7) February
8) 3 Musketeers
9) 3
10) 15
11) 3.29 ounces, 93.3 grams

PAGES 19-20

1) True
2) True
3) d) San Diego
4) 12
5) "The Magic Isle"
6) San Diego California and Vicinity (take credit for "San Diego")
7) M
8) San Diego California and Vicinity (take credit for "San Diego")
9) 4
10) 4
11) Highway, Empire
12) Yosemite National Park (take credit for "Yosemite"), Los Angeles

PAGES 21-22

1) False
2) Red
3) Spin
4) b) 400
5) 500; dark blue
6) 20; dark blue
7) O
8) 100
9) 22
10) d, b, a, c

PAGES 23-24

1) True
2) False
3) Red
4) Park Place
5) 3
6) 6 AM-9 AM
7) Skateboarding, rollerblading
8) 3rd Monday
9) a) right-hand pole; b) left-hand pole; c) center pole
10) 15
11) Orange (or yellow), green, blue, red
12) 4100
13) "distinguishing placards"
14) 4
15) 2; to the left

PAGES 25–26
1) False
2) Upper Minnie Mouse tin
3) Blue, white
4) "Öööhhhm"
5) Minnie Mouse, Donald Duck; Donald Duck's is written in blue
6) Upper Minnie Mouse tin
7) 2
8) Upper Goofy tin, lower Donald Duck tin
9) Starburst, cloud, cloud, starburst
10) Lower Mickey Mouse tin
11) Upper Minnie Mouse tin, lower Goofy tin
12) 5

PAGES 27–28
1) True
2) b) Clif Bar
3) $2.60
4) 4
5) Peanut butter crackers, Fig Bar
6) Chipper
7) Lorna Doone, SnackWell's, Oreo (take credit for "SnackWell" since it's partly obscured)
8) 205
9) Cranberry Almond Delight, Yogurt Apple Nut Mix
10) Knott's Berry Farm

PAGES 29–30
1) False
2) d) French
3) 16
4) "Chemistry – Comparative Biochemistry"
5) 6
6) "Etomology"
7) 33
8) 5
9) 9
10) Chemistry, Economics, Education
11) "Engineering, Electrical"

PAGES 31–32
1) True
2) 9
3) "How to Die Before Your Time"
4) Addressograph
5) "Eat starches."
6) "Kechoo"
7) K
8) a) undertaker; b) dumb birds
9) d) The waiter is holding a plate in his right hand and the man is holding a fork in his right hand
10) Avoid
11) 17
12) 13

PAGES 33–34
1) True
2) 8
3) 1 to 18, Even
4) Green
5) 17, 18
6) 22
7) 25
8) White
9) Serie
10) 26
11) 10, 31
12) 23/24/26/27
13) 8
14) 19
15) 33, 20

PAGES 35–36
1) False
2) b) Christina Aguilera
3) Road & Track
4) c) Miley's Boy Toy
5) Power
6) a) Street Rodder; b) Triathlete; c) Life & Style; d) Digital Photo Pro (take credit for "Photo Pro")
7) 5
8) 4
9) a) 50; b) 550; c) 89; d) 49

PAGES 37–38
1) False
2) Yellow
3) Sciatic nerve
4) Colon
5) Shoulder, arm
6) a) left; b) left; c) right; d) right; e) right
7) Sinuses
8) Pelvis
9) Spleen
10) Esophagus
11) Heart (earth), spine (pines)

PAGES 39–40
1) True
2) Green
3) "a male and a female orangutan"
4) "feeding platform"
5) 4
6) Kira-kira
7) Please
8) Jangan
9) 8
10) Bersama
11) Guide, meter

PAGES 41–42
1) False
2) b) Baghdad
3) Date line
4) 18
5) Caracas
6) 7
7) Africa
8) Peking, Hong Kong, Manila; Paris, Geneva, Rome
9) Noumea
10) Tokyo
11) 22

PAGES 43–44
1) True
2) "Pull ahead to order"
3) Guacamole, Swiss, bacon
4) 9
5) BK minis
6) Tendergrill Chicken Sandwich
7) $1.00
8) BK Double Stacker, BK Triple Stacker
9) BK Big Fish
10) $6.79
11) 3
12) A1 Steakhouse XT

PAGES 45–46
1) True
2) False
3) Will Smith
4) Tom Bradley
5) c) left foot
6) a) September 24, 1981; b) April 30, 2011; c) August 7, 1941
7) a) your success; b) Ted; c) made this all possible; d) 50 great
8) Norma Talmadge
9) Douglas Fairbanks, Will Smith
10) Barbara Stanwyck, Robert Taylor

PAGES 47–48
1) True
2) 9
3) Pemberton
4) 3
5) Basket
6) One Mile Lake
7) 6
8) Bear-proof
9) Heart
10) Wait your turn, Do not litter
11) South
12) admin@pemberton.ca, 604.894.6135
13) $8,975

PAGES 49–50
1) False
2) International Herald Tribune
3) Tuesday
4) Belgium
5) €2.50
6) Shield
7) £5
8) a) hospital dash; b) Baby joy; c) wind farm
9) Indigo (take credit for blue or purple)
10) Vermeer
11) "Royal souvenir special"
12) Monarch

PAGES 51–52
1) False
2) Vertical
3) Left
4) 13:03
5) Red
6) 5p, 10p, 20p, 50p, £1
7) "Rejected coins"
8) "Press for ticket"
9) 8:30 am–6:30 pm
10) c) a vehicle is not parked fully in a marked bay
11) £8 (4 hours at £1 for each 30 minutes)
12) 5 asterisks; 7 bullets
13) Wheelclamped
14) Zone A2
15) Autoslot
16) "inside of windscreen"

PAGES 53–54
1) False
2) d) Goofy
3) Thank You
4) Both $1.99 (Money/Gift Card Holder, For the Graduate)
5) Cat
6) a) prosperity; b) made me so happy; c) In Your New Home
7) Workplace, Humor
8) Bat Mitzvah, Bar Mitzvah
9) a) Thank You; b) Achievement; c) New Home; d) Congratulations
10) "A Retirement Wish For Someone Special"

PAGES 55–56
1) False (Alberta also appears)
2) Indian
3) Colorado
4) 34 cents
5) California
6) Green; in the lower right corner
7) USA
8) "full before and after delivery"
9) Wyoming, Iowa, North Dakota; the other truck plate is from Illinois
10) Puerto Rico, Nebraska, Indiana
11) a) 4PQL179
12) c, a, b, d

PAGES 57–58
1) True
2) "Viva Kennedy"
3) c) Gary Hart
4) Clinton, Gore
5) teddy bear
6) a) Elvis Presley; b) Washington Redskins; c) astronauts; d) Santa Claus
7) a) Peace; b) lever pals; c) loser; d) 60's
8) Humphrey, Kennedy
9) a, b

PAGES 59–60
1) False
2) Xcaret
3) Marruecos
4) Hawaii
5) China
6) Green
7) Xel Há, Grecia
8) White
9) India; 14251 km, 8855 mi
10) Alemania

PAGES 61–62
1) False
2) d) two, on opposite cheeks (the woman in the fedora in the foreground and the man in the yellow cap in the background)
3) a) 2; b) 3; c) 1
4) White
5) a) the leftmost one; b) the leftmost one; c) the second one from the left
6) Brazil, U.S.A.
7) Middle finger
8) Blue, yellow, red, green

PAGES 63–64
1) True
2) Moose
3) a) right; b) left; c) left; d) left; e) left
4) Rotterdam, New York
5) 3
6) Elizabeth Tower (take credit for "Big Ben" or "Clock Tower")
7) 2
8) Berlin, Brazil, Canada, Hawaii, London, Moscow, Nevada
9) Australia, Japan, Las Vegas
10) 14
11) Israel

PAGES 65–66
1) True
2) The left side (see indicator light in center of display)
3) 23°C
4) 5
5) 3
6) P
7) The left side (see indicator in the lower right)
8) 1076
9) 240
10) 750 rpm
11) 7 and 8
12) Chef

PAGES 67–68
1) True
2) a) elastic
3) Yellow, black
4) a) far right; b) far left; c) far left; d) far right
5) Elastic
6) 2
7) 10
8) White, yellow, pink, orange, green, red
9) 4
10) Dark green
11) 12

PAGES 69–70
1) True
2) Red
3) 6
4) Triangle, xylophone
5) Green
6) Green
7) Yellow
8) a) 2 and 3; b) 4; c) 2; d) 1
9) Flower, house
10) Green, purple, pink
11) Light green

PAGES 71–72
1) False
2) Bananas
3) "Corporate Development"
4) 1900–2000
5) 3
6) J. Smith
7) Red
8) Sunflower
9) d) "Practical Reference"
10) "Birds Encyclopedia"
11) 2010
12) "Philosophy of Life"
13) "Equipment & Technologies"
14) "Modern Architecture"
15) "n Design"

PAGES 73–74
1) True
2) True
3) False
4) d) paintbrush
5) 7
6) 2 pairs
7) Dark blue (take credit if you thought that color was black)
8) a) paint; b) car; c) screen door
9) Laundry, Vacuum
10) Work gloves, sponge, scrubbing brush, screwdriver
11) Nails

PAGES 75–76
1) False
2) c) Pineapple smoothie
3) Mango, guava, coconut
4) Pineapple
5) 3
6) b) diamond
7) Chai
8) No smoking
9) 5
10) Lemonade

PAGES 77–78
1) False
2) 5–0
3) a) left; b) right; c) right
4) Nationals
5) Bottom of the fourth inning
6) Lower left
7) a) Jason Bay; b) 44; c) .250; d) second inning; e) fly out
8) Bob's Discount Furniture, Subway
9) 9
10) 8
11)
12) 3
13) rplequipment.com

PAGES 79–80
1) True
2) Upper left
3) a) Dr Pepper
4) Hackberry General Store
5) Pegasus, gargoyle
6) Furthest left: b (Route U.S. 66); furthest right: d (Route US 66 National Historic Highway); uppermost: a (Route 66)
7) Pop, Ice, Snacks, Souvenirs
8) Royal Triton
9) Corvette
10) 1 (in the background near the gas pump)

PAGES 81–82
1) True
2) $4
3) 7; 2 have monocles
4) 9
5) 3
6) a) both are packaged in cardboard boxes
7) 5
8) b) to its left
9) 9, 12, 16, 22
10) 9, 26
11) Stuffed Nemo dolls, Fly-Sky Bat
12) Blue dog, pink dog, blue dog, red dragon, orange bear, white cat, orange bear, red dragon, orange bear, red dragon

PAGES 83–84
1) False
2) a) scissors
3) Glasses, smartphone, pencil
4) Blue, red
5) 6
6) Development Diversity
7) 7; yellow
8) V
9) Green, purple
10) c, d, a, b
11) Fullwidth, Boxed
12) 7

PAGES 85–86
1) False
2) Tom Bradley
3) a-x: EVA Air, b-z: Fiji Airways, c-y: Japan Airlines
4) ANA, KLM, LAN
5) 7, 9, 7, 8
6) Air Tahiti Nui
7) Aeroflot, Turkish Airlines
8) Emirates
9) Philippine
10) Saudia, Singapore, Swiss

PAGES 87–88
1) True
2) False
3) a) mobilised; b) W; c) how, has, her
4) The second (middle) one
5) Bombs
6) R is smaller than the rest; D is surrounded by the belt
7) French
8) 2
9) High Explosives, Heavy Guns
10) National Projectile Factories
11) 3 before the war; 100 working today
12) 8

PAGES 89–90
1) False
2) $3.469, $3.589, $3.719
3) "All taxes included"
4) $15.58
5) Super
6) "No Smoking Stop Engine"
7) 89
8) 10%
9) "Prepay inside"
10) 5
11) $75
12) Yellow, green, red, blue
13) "Select Product"

PAGES 91–92
1) True
2) "Edwards Canyon Country 10"
3) 3
4) Popcorn (yellow), candy (red), ice cream (blue)
5) "The Pyramid"
6) "Exodus: Gods and Kings" and "The Penguins of Madagascar"
7) Yellow
8) "Interstellar"
9) 5
10) 12:40, 3:00, 10:35

PAGES 93–94
1) True
2) EC
3) Dark hair
4) "Non resident"
5) 12
6) Ohio, Massachusetts
7) Massachusetts
8) To the right
9) Ohio
10) 3
11) 4
12) New Mexico, New York
13) Rhode Island, 132-465
14) Kentucky

PAGES 95–96
1) False
2) True
3) Orange (take credit if you thought that color was yellow)
4) 4 and 7
5) 6
6) Africa
7) a) ♋ (Pisces)
8) c) man holding a mirror
9) a, c, d, b
10) 17
11) 2 and 11

PAGES 97–98
1) True
2) Bottom
3) Cat, Bud
4) EcoBoost
5) 1
6) Peak
7) Five
8) Pudding
9) 27, 29, 38
10) 22, 31

PAGES 99–100
1) True
2) Thursday
3) "No SIM"
4) 44%
5) e) Stocks
6) 280
7) A heart
8) 114
9) App Store
10) Voice Memos
11) Contacts, Camera

PAGES 101–102
1) True
2) a) "Sunny Afternoon";
   b) "Women on the Verge of a
   Nervous Breakdown"; c) "King
   Charles III"
3) A, R, N, N
4) b) the one with a leopard-skin
   coat
5) Tape over his mouth
6) a) compulsory; b) goosebumps;
   c) crowning achievement;
   d) great British musical;
   e) joyous
7) 0844 482 5120
8) 27 red stars, 22 black stars
9) Funny, stylish, well-performed,
   quirky
10) Tamsin Greig, Haydn Gwynne

PAGES 103–104
1) True
2) 12
3) 255
4) 203
5) 258
6) 328
7) 205, 208
8) 256
9) 308
10) 233, 237
11) 303, 310

PAGES 105–106
1) Black; green
2) 18
3) Hearts; king (of clubs)
4) 11
5) 4
6) 19
7) Ten; 21
8) Jack of diamonds
9) Two
10) Eight

PAGES 107–108
1) True
2) False
3) 11
4) d) PLED
5) F
6) Line 7
7) b) You can see some of his top
   teeth, but none of his bottom
   teeth
8) Lines 8 and 9
9) D
10) FDPLTCEO

PAGES 109–110
1) False
2) Bensons
3) April 1, 2011
4) a) red
5) Noël Coward, New Players,
   Novello
6) Novello, Noël Coward, New
   Players
7) Ground
8) 2
9) London Transport Museum
10) Edgware Road, Marylebone
11) Ambassadors, St. Martin's
12) b) Floral Street
13) a, c

PAGES 111–112
1) True
2) False
3) To the right
4) d, a, c, b
5) a) terminal machinery;
   b) C.C.T.V.; c) gate house;
   d) hi-visibility; e) cranes
6) Boots, vest, gloves
7) Yellow crane paths, yellow
   pedestrian walkways
8) 2
9) C, L
10) 4

PAGES 113–114
1) False
2) Light blue
3) Two 5's
4) 100
5) 5
6) Pennsylvania, Short Line
7) Green, orange
8) a) Free Parking; b) B. & O.
   Railroad; c) Income Tax (take
   credit for "Income" since it's
   partly obscured); d) In Jail/Just
   Visiting (take credit for "Jail")
9) "Pay poor tax of $15"
10) Virginia Avenue, States Avenue;
    the others are Boardwalk and
    Park Place

PAGES 115–116

1) False
2) February 25
3) Brussels, Johannesburg; A15 or B43
4) "Flight closing"
5) Prague, Munich, Berlin
6) c) Istanbul
7) Nice
8) F
9) New York, Hong Kong, Tel Aviv
10) 19:50
11) 20:15, 07:00
12) Aberdeen
13) Dubai

PAGES 117–118

1) False
2) a) 4 and 5; b) 1 and 2; c) 10 and 11
3) A colander
4) The son, in his left hand
5) Red and blue
6) d) the right-hand photo, tilting right
7) Yellow
8) 6
9) a) facing each other
10) a, d
11) c, a, d, b

PAGES 119–120

1) False
2) 118.00
3) GPS, IFR
4) 50
5) Detection
6) 2 and 3
7) Test
8) WPT, FPL
9) "Prop lever – feather"
10) 30

PAGES 121–122

1) True
2) c) Don't forget to feed the birds
3) 8
4) a) tomorow (tomorrow); b) to (two); c) Samanta (Samantha); d) no misspelled word; e) Upgent (Urgent)
5) 3
6) a) yellow; b) red; c) lavender; d) green; e) orange
7) 4; they are not all the same color
8) 6
9) "Listen to your heart"

PAGES 123–124

1) False
2) www.LondonTheatreBookings.com
3) a-w, b-y, c-x, d-z
4) Left
5) "Official agent"
6) a) Left; b) Right; c) Right; d) Right; e) Left
7) Pride
8) Ladders
9) Madame Tussauds
10) "Billy Elliot"

PAGES 125–126

1) True
2) "Won't be beat"
3) a, c, b; c is ravioli
4) Natural
5) Cappola
6) c) 2 × 175 g
7) $3.00
8) Main Street
9) Cheddar
10) 6

PAGES 127–128

1) False
2) True
3) False
4) 7
5) 407
6) 4 and 5
7) 419
8) 4
9) a) inn operator; b) try to investigate; c) seal with wet towels
10) 422, 423
11) 435, 437
12) Elevators, evacuation, exit, extinguishers
13) 416, 418, 426, 428, 434

PAGES 129–130

1) False
2) K
3) I
4) Wham
5) Dire Straits in red, Tears for Fears in yellow
6) c) Iva Zaniochi
7) d) "Dancing in the Street"
8) C3, C4, E9, E0
9) Donna Summer, Chris Isaak, David Lee Roth
10) polka, mazurka, beguine
11) Casadei

PAGES 131–132

1) True
2) January 26
3) b) Gordon
4) a) a solid square
5) Green
6) Hat, heart, horse
7) 5
8) ADS
9) 4, 8, 2, 3
10) L
11) parade, favorite

PAGES 133–134
1) False
2) a) Africa
3) Droom
4) Romantic
5) b) New Jersey
6) Hat, Adventurers
7) Yay
8) Laugh (laughter)
9) Welcome
10) Peace
11) Green

PAGES 135–136
1) False
2) Right
3) Arthur Flegenheimer
4) Schultz, Harmon
5) 1934
6) "Federal Income Tax Law"
7) SPring 7–3100 (777-3100)
8) 31
9) 5 feet, 7 inches; 165 pounds
10) brown, gray
11) F.
12) 50149

PAGES 137–138
1) True
2) c) Washington Monument
3) 3
4) Ontario Place
5) Elephant
6) Adirondacks
7) Blue
8) Statue of Liberty
9) Robot
10) Walt Disney World
11) Nelson, Helen, Nadine, Luigi
12) Ace of spades, ace of diamonds
13) Midland, Ontario

PAGES 139–140
1) True
2) Blue, green, black, yellow
3) c) 37g
4) 3
5) "Amount Per Serving"
6) Protein
7) Vitamin E; black; 30%
8) 95mg
9) 5g
10) 480
11) Trans

PAGES 141–142
1) True
2) c) The Addams Family
3) Antz, Sylvester & Tweety
4) Maurice; The Flintstones
5) Fall of the Foot Clan (visible in two places)
6) a) Maniacs; b) Pinball; c) 21; d) Schlümpfe
7) Tetris, Tennis
8) Paperboy
9) WWF Raw (take credit for "Raw")

PAGES 143–144
1) True
2) Red
3) $10
4) 18
5) $17,000
6) T, B, C
7) 33, 21, 7, 35
8) Rainbow
9) 448,000
10) calottery.com/REPLAY
11) 23, 24, 11, 30, 29, 25

PAGES 145–146
1) False
2) Bello
3) NBC
4) Hell's Kitchen
5) "In the Heights"
6) Incredible
7) "Phantom (of the Opera)"
8) Medieval Times
9) Toys "R" Us
10) a) Look Up; b) Groovaloo; c) Artifact

PAGES 147–148
1) False
2) c) Asiago Cheese
3) Owl
4) A dollop
5) Steamer
6) 3
7) Cinnamon buns
8) Mixed Berry, Chocolate
9) Cream cheese, capers, and veggies
10) $1.51
11) 4 (Espresso, Cappuccino, Americano, Macchiato)
12) b, d, c, a

PAGES 149–150
1) True
2) c) Marines
3) a) Hare Krishna; b) president; c) Inland; d) party; e) Creations; f) drive badly
4) 1-800-BE-ALERT (If you decided to translate that into numbers, that's impressive but you didn't need to do it)
5) Dodgers
6) 95.5
7) Three figures with green hair
8) "It's been Monday all week!"

PAGES 151–152
1) True
2) Four
3) Break, space
4) 10
5) Copy
6) Verify
7) 9
8) B; bin, border, bright
9) Peek
10) Graphics
11) Step, dim

PAGES 153–154
1) True
2) a) Martin Short
3) "Orange Is the New Black," "Wild"
4) Heather
5) a) Loneliness; b) Blood; c) Heaven; d) the Turtle
6) "I Am Malala"
7) $25
8) 6
9) Thomas (Matthew Thomas, Thomas King)
10) Yellow
11) Soup Sisters, Broth Brothers

PAGES 155–156
1) False
2) a) up
3) Kiribati
4) Singapura
5) 3
6) 25
7) Isle of Man
8) Beatrix, Juliana
9) a, d, b, c
10) DFW
11) 1996

PAGES 157–158
1) True
2) The Greek Theatre
3) Two
4) Tom Petty & the Heartbreakers
5) a) The Circle Tour; b) The Eclipse Tour; c) Time Machine Tour
6) In the middle of the right-hand column
7) livenation.com
8) Mark & Brian Christmas Show
9) U
10) Van Halen, Kool & the Gang
11) c) 718465537616

PAGES 159–160
1) a) right; b) left; c) left; d) right
2) Mondays
3) 1, 7
4) Your
5) Barclays (upper right), HSBC (upper middle), Morgan Stanley (lower left)
6) "Jersey Boys"
7) Amar'e Stoudemire
8) 10
9) 4
10) 2092

PAGES 161–162
1) False
2) 71
3) Dixon; 7th hole
4) Clarke, Park
5) "Match No / Tee Time"
6) M.
7) 5
8) 24
9) Kamte
10) Jonzon; 64
11) Larsen
12) Gonzalez

PAGES 163–164
1) Uncle Ben's
2) a) Chicken noodle
3) Contadina
4) Cream of mushroom
5) Spiced cider
6) Pecans
7) a) top; b) top; c) bottom; d) bottom; e) middle; f) middle
8) Traditional
9) Authentic Texas recipe
10) 6

PAGES 165–166
1) False
2) a) "bacon"
3) "sag"
4) "two"
5) "language"
6) "repulsive"
7) "my"
8) "above," "blow," "stare"
9) "symphony"
10) d, a, c, b

Image Credits